T0105535

So, What's Wrong, Black Man?

"A truthful eye-opening and mind-blowing view of the problems that plague the Black man and his community with an opinionated solution to his growing concerns."

By
James Reid

Order this book online at www.trafford.com
or email orders@trafford.com

Most Trafford titles are also available at major online book retailers.

Printed in the United States of America.

ISBN: 978-1-4269-3585-5 (sc)
ISBN: 978-1-4269-3586-2 (e-b)

*Our mission is to efficiently provide the world's finest, most comprehensive book publishing
service, enabling every author to experience success. To find out how to publish your book, your
way, and have it available worldwide, visit us online at www.trafford.com*

Trafford rev. 08/04/2010

 www.trafford.com

North America & international
toll-free: 1 888 232 4444 (USA & Canada)
phone: 250 383 6864 ♦ fax: 812 355 4082

Foreword by: Audrey E. Giles, Bishop

This book gives a wake up call to the world. Why the world? Because we live among every kind of human being that we feel we can blame for any or all our mistakes. I have seized the moment of this book in every area of our African American men, the good, the bad and the ugly. We may feel that the system has failed us and it had at times, but we have failed ourselves by not bring responsible for our actions. Your choices are who you are. So, What's wrong Black man points that out. It's a seller.

Bishop Audrey E. Giles
By God's Grace Ministries Inc.
Beacon, NY

Foreword by: Dr. James J. Fedderman; Asst. Principal & Educator

I have always wanted to become an educator and an educational administrator, both of which I have accomplished. However, the various issues and laws that have negatively dictated many decisions that have the potential to further break components of an already fragile generation are more noticeable today than ever. Many thoughts have surfaced that suggest why society is currently oppressed and depressed, but the separation of church and state limits the amount of conversation that would be deemed appropriate. This book encapsulates real issues that plague Black America, which inhibits our own people from making progress, but others are seemingly the blame for our own transgressions in which we ourselves are the major contributors often times. I encourage every black man and black woman to pick up this book and read what is written. This book will open the thinking mind of those who desire to gain truth, knowledge and understanding to the problems that black men face each and every day in this country and give simple, down to earth examples and solutions that will propel us into a great community of people.

James J. Fedderman, Ph.D.
Accawmacke Elementary School
Daughtery, Va.

Table of Contents

Introduction by: James A Reid

Some of my family members and friends have said to me, James, why are writing this book and why did you give it a title called, "So, what's wrong Black man?" and my reply to such a question was this. I'm writing this book simply because I love my black people and I want to voice my view in the form of words on how I see the black community as a whole today. In addition, I want their eyes to be open to hope once again and not closed to the devastation that were targeted against us and what we are causing one another ourselves. I want my people to be educated in not only book knowledge, but have a better understanding of life itself. And I want my people to unite together in black love by the extension of their hand to uplift the next Black woman or man. And as far as the title goes, it's a question that no matter where you are in life, we all can do something positive that will better our lives' and the lives' of those in our community and all around us. It's a title that every Black man should ask himself when he sees all the wrong that is taking place within his community and hopefully it will ignite a fire in his soul that will inspire him to realize that hope begins with him wanting to bring about change. I hope that it is a titled question that will awaken the conscience and compassion of a great people that is sick and tired of the aftermath that is the residue stain leftover from all the violence, the drug selling, the high school dropout rate and teen pregnancy that we are experiencing. Let us get back to knowing that the only time that we should look down on a man or a woman is to lift them up and help brush them off. This is a book that is solely to inform; encourage; empower; equip and uplift the Black man and anyone else who would like to gain another perspective by broaden their mind. It's a book about the view of the black community as a whole from the eyes of a man who has not always made the right decisions in life, but, by the grace and mercy of ALMIGHTY GOD, he now see life in a whole new light and he is someone who is tired of seeing his people not being honest with themselves when it comes to their condition. Someone who is tired of seeing his people last in everything good like health care, finance, education and job creation. But first in every area in society that is bad. From all the senseless killing to robbing, to the selling of drugs, to degrading one another in words and song. Than blaming it on Slavery, the White man; the Country and every other excuse they can come up with and not stepping in front of a mirror and say to that person that he or she is facing that I can no longer blame others for my present day failures. It's a book on how we can become the change we hope to see not only in the community in which we live, but the black community as a whole. A book that has the potential power to change how black folks view themselves and a rough draft opinion on what it will take for them to get back to that proud race that has conquered every obstacle that they have come up against by the way of their strong belief in Almighty GOD, Family, Heritage and a Commitment to achieve and overcome. I hope that it's a book that will bring the black community closer together as a people rather than to keep them separated as so many are today. Some of the words and statements made in this book hopefully will cause the reader to step back and give his or her situation or circumstance a hard look and hopefully say to him or herself, what can I do to bring about change in my community and that of myself? It is not intended to cause a ripple effect or widen the gap between Black's and White's, but to give a clear cut reason to why some may think and act the way they do on both sides. It is a rough draft to once we know that the trap has been laid for the bird (Black People) and we come to the knowledge and understanding of how it works, than we should use that information to our advantage and not conduct ourselves in the actions that the trapper (White man) expects us to act. It will show how the system that is in place was carefully crafted to make Black people think that they are inferior to White people and White people are superior to Black people by way of the Educational system; the Justice system and the Economic system. It will show that through these systems, Black people have been culturally condition to think, act and view themselves in a certain way. It will give insight to show how poverty and economic hardship was systematically placed in the Black neighborhoods to keep the Black man in the proximity of his slave ancestor as much as possible. It will show how the Black man will graciously accept this burden and place blame on everyone else by walking in the traps laid before him that he refuses to gain knowledge of, than cry wolf once he's caught. This book is not design to place all blame on the White man, for only we can stop ourselves and there were and still are thousand's of goodhearted decent White people in America that gave their lives' by speaking out against the treatment of the negro man in this country. Hopefully, it's a book that will open our eyes and band Black men's together with determination; courage and heart, which will propel us beyond the White man's opinion of us and the opinion we have of ourselves. And above all, it's a book that will instruct us to restore black pride back in our community and accept responsibility for the very actions we commit and not blame and fault others for our failures. And once we can come to grips with that truth, with that reality, than we just might have the courage that Almighty GOD has placed in us, to say to our Love one's; our Preacher's and Minister's; our Teacher's; our Community leaders and above all, OURSELVES that simple, but powerful question; SO, WHAT'S WRONG BLACK MAN? And not be afraid of the answer that will follow; The answer is="ME"

Ch. 1 - Education:
A raw look at a broken system

This is the question I have of me, is a Black man in this country really free? What a question for you to ask yourself, but here's one that is perhaps more profound than that and here it is, in live and living words; So, what's wrong Black man? Let that sink in for a minuet, cause by the end of this book, you will be asking yourself this question over and over again. It is a powerful question that every Black man should ask himself as he do a 360 around his plotted space, step back and take a hard look at all the wrong that he has accepted, succumb to and adopted, and not be afraid of the answer that may follow such a question that demands HIS answer. He must see the problems that plague his community and no longer be blind to such reality and negativity that goes on there. He must realize that if he is not the solution to the condition of his community, than he is part of its problem by continuing his way of thinking and waiting for someone else to solve the problem that he is to some degree creating and/or allowing to prosper. The Black man must somehow come to grips with the reality that he can no longer sit on his ass with his hands tied behind his back singing Kumbaya while his people continue being broken in spirit and wounded in soul. But, who am I to say something about his people? One of the biggest problems that face the Black man is that he has yet to grow beyond his enslaved mind as a whole and his fear to be more than the opinion that the White man may have of him. The White man has always had an opinion of the Black man as for as his intellect goes, and the young blacks forfeit their GOD given intellect by dropping out or not going to school, thus living out the opinion the White man have of them and that opinion is now their reality. The young black male along with the young black female continue in this mindset that had been repeated over and over again by the children of the slave masters of old for hundreds of years and what makes it so bad is that we pass it on to our young children and not realizing the damage that we are causing by the destructive pattern that we have so proudly accepted and we smile while we do it. Look at how the Black man has been program down through the years and what I mean by this is that the Black man has been culturally condition to think and act a certain way since the beginning of slavery. He has not escaped his slave mentality even after Lincoln signed the Emancipation Proclamation that freed his ancestors more than four hundred years ago. Now, this statement may make some of you mad and upset with me and if it does, so be it, but I will speak the truth on how I see my beautiful Black people and I will not attempt to find an excuse for my statement, but perhaps give you a reason to why I'm making it. Take a minute and look at the actions of our Black youth today and their view on education and school. Young girls are skipping classes just to run off and have sex with boys just to brag that they are no longer virgins. They are getting themselves pregnant at an alarming rate; polluting the community with STD's and they lead with a higher percentage rate for contracting HIV or AIDS and they care nothing for the lesson of the day. The drop out rate among young juveniles between the ages of 14-16 years of age is at a staggering height and todays black youth for the most part cannot read on a 5th. Grade level and those that can are so distracted with the street business of the day, (Gang activity; Drugs; Violence; Sex; etc.etc.) that they can't stay focus enough to absorb that in which they have read or that which is being taught at the time by the teacher or instructor, but they can flow-out a rhyme to a song that they have heard only once and swear up and down that they are the greatest thing to come along in the rap game since the discovery of Jay-Z. They rather choose jail and prison by their actions than to attend college; they rather pick-up a handgun to jack up some old lady than to pick up an application for a job; They rather read about the life and times of Jay-Z; P. Diddy; Snoop Dogg and 50 cent, than to read about The Mis-education of the Negro by Carter G. Woodson, not knowing that most of these Negro rappers to some degree don't give a damn about them or their community for if they did, they would have spoke up against the injustice like that which happen down in Jena, Louisiana with the Jena 6. Now I'm not saying to a true fact that those I just mention don't have organizations that they've started and perhaps fund with their own money to better the lives' of people, but what I am saying is that some of these rappers can do a better job in promoting education, responsibility, respect of one's self and others, sharing, giving back and taking pride in their community. Many of our young people look at these rappers as some type of god and these rappers knows it. I do believe that if someone like Jay-Z, 50 cents or some other rapper would come out and tell these young kids that education is the way to go, than in my opinion, they will have a new view to the importance of education. Tell them to help one another in the community by volunteering to clean up their neighborhoods and stop using the "N" word, than I'm sure that many of our young people will take hold of that and run with it. However, they must also let them know that if they choose not to do anything like this, they do not want their support. By putting that positive message in their rap and in their videos, I believe that the education rate among young black boys will begin to grow. But who am I fooling, these guys put money before their own people and make their millions from the destruction that they themselves help promote. There's a quote by India's late philosopher Mahatma Gandhi that goes like this **(The best way to find yourself is to lose yourself in the service of others.)** Rappers like a Jay-Z can energize our young people in the area of service rather than an area of self-centernish. The education system in this country has brain washed our children so bad that they think that it is more important to read a Source or Vibe magazine about hip-hop, than to read about the REAL FREEDOM FIGHTER'S like Martin Luther King; Medger Evers; Fredrick Douglas; Malcolm X; Harriet Tubman; Shirley Chisum or Sojourner Truth, not knowing that these folks gave their lives' so that they could be who they are today, but once again, Who am I to say something about his people? They rather hang out on the street corner calling one another" NIGGER" and let me make it more fashionable for today's terminology and street language," NIGGA" with their pants down below their ass that they think that by dropping the "ER" at the end of the word and adding the "A" changes the meaning of the word. They have fallen victim to the White man's game because the White man no longer have to call the Black man "Nigger" anymore do to the simple fact that THEY call one another that constantly. They have taking on the cultural conditioning of the old slave master by not wanting to be educated with the fear of the whip that is in the slave master's hand that once broke the spirit of their ancestors to learn. That whip now being an educated mind. Sometimes I wander if our young black kids even want to become smart, I do not know. Than they think that by dropping out of school and pursuing a Thug's life, that they are really sticking it to the MAN as if that's something to boast about. Both the young Black man and the old Black man has brought shame to his ancestor's suffering and death by not wanting to educate himself or his children. And by not extending a helping hand to uplift the next Black man out of his condition, than how do we ever come together as a people United as One and fueled by LOVE. However, by choosing the path that was led down for him to travel, he continues to forward the destructive demise of the Black man and he has welcomed it with open arms, open heart and an open mind. But, once again, Who am I to say something about his people? They degrade and demean their heritage, their history and one another with their words, their dress and their actions. Many choose not having any interest in broadening their sense of purpose by expanding their beautiful minds and their vocabulary. He has not flourish beyond that human conditioning that has been woven into his DNA down through the years. He has been culturally condition by means of Education; Television, Radio; History; Community and Economics. Talk show radio host personality, Joe Madison makes this statement daily on his radio show, Power 169 on XM satellite radio. He states that in this country, we are culturally condition to believe, that WHITE is SURPERIOR, BLACK is INFERIOR and the manifestation of that cultural conditioning is that, Black people are Undervalued; Underestimated and Marginalized. Let's take a quick look at his statement, dating back to the days of slavery and see the relevance of it today. Black people has always been Undervalued to the degree that they was called" NIGGER" by the slave master's to show that the color of his skin made him to be of no value other than that of a slave. And in the eyes of most slave owners back then and to some folks even today, the Black man is still considered lower than cattle, but a little higher than a flea infested dog. He was Underestimated because he was kept from learning, thus making him not smart enough in the eyes of the slave master to achieve anything beyond the faded memories of his past. And his expectations to achieve was broken by the way of the whip, the separation of his family and the kidnapping of him from his native home. He was Marginalized more so because he was excluded and ignored with no importance than that of any other nationality of people back then and too some, even so now. And why wouldn't I want my Black people to continue on this path? Simple, we are a better people than that. Why do our young blacks dishonor so many souls by refusing to finish school and not only that, not attend? They refuse to vote once they become of age, because they believe the lie that their vote does not count and it does not make a difference, but yet, they accept the shame they bring to their people by fulfilling the wishes and the agenda of the White man. And I will say it again, "So, what's wrong Black man?" Ask yourself what is wrong. If we will take the time and read our history, we will see that education was high on the mind of most slaves. They were denied learning and some lost their lives for even attempting to learn how to read, but yet, some, even after having their backs lashed with whips and chains continued to learn secretly by some goodhearted white folks, not many, but some, because they knew that in order to have a future, not only for themselves, but more important for their children, they had to learn, because they knew that in order to overcome slavery and the disadvantage that was place before them, they had to educate themselves just to try to level the playing field, maybe not during their life time, but perhaps in years to come. If you are one of those folks who thinks that this is not a true statement, than tell me who is the nation's president and what color is He? And I also believe that a educated man is a powerful man and a educated Black man is not only a powerful man, but a cultural changer. Does Dr. Martin Luther King come to mind, for who changed cultural more than he other than Jesus Christ Himself? Once a Black man get himself educated and I don't only mean by way of book knowledge, for book knowledge is good, but wisdom by way of experience in my opinion is better and once that knowledge and wisdom come together and he see that in order to build an army, all it takes is for one person to step up who has the willingness to forward change. And this can be achieved by way of renewing his mind in GOD in such a way that he has a new view on life when he see that the chaotic action of the black youth is a reflection of him. However, if he chooses to do nothing to correct the actions that has affected him and left him in the state of denial to see that there is a problem among his people, than he too is the problem. But once he accept the mission that GOD has purposed in his heart to do, and he refuse to sit on the back porch any longer with his mouth wired shut and his hands tied down, but has given way to a purpose that is higher than himself, than will he spring to his feet with a new sense of Black pride and power that will make those around him see his passion towards education and community change to wander, what is going on with this guy? And I will tell you what is going on with him. He has accepted his calling and is no longer afraid to let the inner change that has taking place within him to be bound, but expressed outwardly for all to see. Than he will speak with that boldness; that passion; that fire and the soul of a Kingly people that has brought forth the strongest nation of people that has ever walked this great Earth of ours to victory and say; I WILL NOT GO QUIETLY IN THE NIGHT; I WILL NOT SURRENDER WITHOUT A FIGHT; I WILL MARCH FORWARD TO THE VERY END; I WILL STAND UP FOR BOTH FAMILY AND FRIEND; I WILL NOT TURN BACK, NO NOT NOW, FOR MY EYES HAVE SEEN GOD's GLORY CROWN; HE HAS PROVEN HIMSELF TO BOTH YOU AND ME, FOR THIS BLACK MAN HAS NOW, BEEN SET FREE. My black man friend, only you have the power to stop you, believe that. Most of us who was fortunate enough to have finish high school haven't picked up a book since our last assignment and we fail to realize that reading is one of our most powerful weapons that we have, but again, if WE do not stress the importance of education in our homes, in our churches or meeting place, than how can we as parents or legal guardians expect for our kids to see and understand the importance of it. We do not explain to our young people that black folks have paid a heavy price for just picking up a book back in the day and the price for such an act was the brutal taken of his or her life. But, once again, Who am I to say something about his people? So, what's wrong Black man? Should be the question that roll out of our mouths on a daily basis or at least run across our minds for time to time. We have gotten to the point that our young blacks think that it's a curse to be smart. If a child in school do all the right things to excel in his or her scholastic subjects in school, they are sometimes criticized; ridiculed or picked on for being smart and not to mention if they speak proper English and conduct themselves in an orderly manner, my goodness, they are judged by their peers and are called talking and acting "WHITE", whatever that mean. When a child conducts him or herself in an orderly manner and talk like they have some POSITIVE home training, when did black people vote on that law that it should be categorized as TALKING and ACTING WHITE, because I truly didn't receive my ballot to vote. It's often times considered in the black community that it's not COOL to speak good English, at least among a large population of the black youth in today's society. It's all about talking SLANG or being HIP and the language that is used by today's teens will make Rudy Ray Moore sound like a choir boy, than they wander why they can't get a job. Hell, many times an employer will not hire you simply because you open your mouth. Let me explain. An potential employer can tell a lot about you within the first few words you speak. You cannot be using slang at a job interview and expect to be hired. He or she ask you a question that requires a YES or NO answer and you give them slang. Don't get me wrong, slang has it place and at times, you just cannot use it in every place at any time is what I'm saying. Education in the black community to some degree is not preached as important as it once was back in the day and it's more so in the HOOD, The Projects or The Ghetto as we most know. One of the biggest problems some folks may have with this statement is that it's so very TRUE. Once again, I will make this statement. How can education become important to our black youth if it's not important to US as parents or legal guardians. All we have to do is look around our homes, our community or the house next door, kid's are playing with the video games for hours at a time, they are on the cell phone talking and texting throughout the day and they go to school just to take up space and return home with not one book in their hand. Our kids will pick-up a video game before they will even think about grabbing a book and you know what, we encourage them to do so. We do not ask them if they have homework or any type of assignment that they may have to do. We no longer ask our grade school kids what they learned today. Hell, maybe we want our kids to be Dum and stupid, I do not know, but what I do know is that we need to make our kids put down the cell phones, unplug the T.V. and video game and read a positive book for atleast an hour per day when they return home from school and if that's to hectic, take them to the library once a week and have them to pick out a book that they like and have them to read it and do a report on it

7

at the end of the week and so they do not feel that its unfair, you read the same book also so that you will know what the book is about when they do the report. If you choose to sit on your blessed assurance and do not take the initiative, than you will be doing the same thing that many of our schools are doing to our kids across this country, dummying them down. Many of our black kids, especially the boys have this false belief that they do not need education beyond high school and not to mention anything about college to succeed in life and they back up their claim with the success of some of their favorite sport hero's like Kobe Bryant; Lebron James and Carmelo Anthony. They further their claim with perhaps their strongest proof that you do not have to be a college graduate to make it in life, they will say just look at rappers like 50 cent; T.I.; Eminem; Nelly; LLCool J. and other's. Those guy's made it and I can play ball and/or I can rap just as good as those guy's and this is the false belief that they so passionately accept. And let us not forget our part in this play. We the parents; teachers; minister's; brother's; sister's and friend's play a role in this dummying down of our kids, especially those parents and teachers that do not have a passion in the duty they have chosen. Now, I'm not blaming all teachers and all parents, for there are plenty of good teachers and parents out there, pushing and encouraging their students and kids towards greatness, but what I am saying is that some teachers may see a child who is struggling to learn and rather than giving that child the help that he or she need when that child say that they do not understand the material, they push that child off in some corner in the room, or worst, diagnose them falsely with (Attention Deficit Disorder) A.D.D. for short as if they are Dr. Phil or someone, when that child fall behind the other kids and tell the parents that their child has a learning disorder and this is becoming a growing concern for black kids throughout the nation, and by this, they are left in their respectable corner until the bell ring. But what the teacher should do in my opinion when the child say that they do not understand the lesson is simply this: YOU DO NOT UNDERSTAND IT YET, BUT YOU WILL. This will encourage the child in a way that they couldn't imaging. And this little nugget goes for the parents also. Schools in this country is truly dummying down our black kids by piling them up in classrooms that is extremely over-crowded, giving them out dated text books that they have to sometimes glue together and learn from, having under paid and over worked teachers and pre-historic rules and regulation on how our schools are to be run and administer that is years behind that of Japan, China, Russia, India and other industrialize nations that is or has surpassed the United States in EDUCATION. I want to say this part before I go on about this so-called great country of ours as far as the education system goes. This country and its greed is forever saying that we will be second place to no one as far as education is concern and I can go with that, but how can we educate our kids when college tuition continue to sky rocket each year by double digit percentage rates. Even if our kids have the grades for college, they can't afford to attend. Hell, it may be safe to say that some of our black kids may have the thinking that it's to expensive to be smart and choose not to. Greed in this country is making it impossible for a child to receive a quality education. But our government want our kids to be the best and the brightest. Students are coming out of college with student loans exceeding $50, $75 and sometimes more than a $100,000, but yet in other countries, many of their students attend college for free or for just a fraction of what it cost in this greed infested country. Start saving for your child's education today while they are young and if you perhaps implement what I said earlier about the book reading, who knows, they just might get a full ride on academics alone. Education will be the new currency in the very near future and it will no longer be success as to whom you know, but WHAT YOU KNOW. Many parents do not take the time to go down to the schools, find out what their child is or is not doing and becoming part of their child's education. They refuse to join the local PTA but can join the neighborhood card party every week. They can pay money several days a week at the bingo game, but can't find money to buy their child a book that will expand their mind. They can talk about every thing that is wrong within the black community, but can't find the words to address the solutions that they see everyday within their own household. They blame everyone else for their child's failure in school, but choose not to take their share of the blame when Lil' C is playing Grand Theft Auto from the minuet he arrived home to the time he goes to bed with the remote in his hand and please don't think that I'm going to let baby-girl off the hook, she's on the phone talking about all of the latest gossip that is going on within the IN crowd where she's PRESIDENT. And they can find ampler time to run here and there and for some strange reason, they can't find a small percentage of that time to visit the school inwhich they blame for the mis-education of their son or daughter. But once again, Who am I to say something about his people? Most folks in the black community do not want to hear the TRUTH when it comes to our failed part in the mis-education of our children, simply because it's easier pointing the finger at the school, the teacher, the school broad office, the neighborhood, the janitor, the bus driver, the dog, the goldfish, etc. etc. you get the point. It all boils down to this, EDUCATION has no importance in some of our homes and some of us pass that same mind-set to our children, fulfilling that which was handed down by the slave master. Once we in the black community place EDUCATION and MORAL VALUE near the top of our "What would it take to succeed in life and fortify the black community list", than you may ask yourself, I now know why he made that statement "So, what's wrong Black man?", and the answer is "ME".

Ch. 2 - Television:
The influence of it

Now let us move to the television, that square box that is mounted on the wall of your home or sitting on a stand in the living room. That piece of plastic with all the neat features that shows the images of our hero's and she-ro's. That square box that takes our mind off all the mess a day can bring. That box, if you are like me most nights when I do watch it, end up watching me by putting me to sleep. Now, off the top of my head, I would take a guess that most households in America have at least two television sets in their home and if some of you are like me, you may have one in the bathroom also and I would even go as far as to say that most of our kids have their very own television in their bedrooms. Here lies the problem in the black community and I will make my statement once again so that you will know that it's a statement that you should ask yourself; So, what's wrong Black man?", now for my answer to this very powerful statement and question. Television plays a HUGE role in our lives, especially the black community and this nation as a whole. Millions of folks saw the tragic event that happened on 9/11; millions saw the O.J. trial; hundreds of millions saw the funeral of the King of Pop, Michael Jackson and tens of millions of people around the world tuned in and watched the swearing in of the nation's first elected Black President, Barack Obama. Therefore, as you can see, television plays a pivotal role in our everyday lives both here and abroad. Television has the power to send negative or positive images throughout the world when it comes to the black man and by those images people around the world base their view on those images no matter how unjust their view may be concerning the black man on those very images, thus leaving them to stereotype. Let's take a quick look at how the White media in this country and how it took a ninety-second sound bite of a sermon that was preached by the Reverend Jeremiah Wright out of total context. Now in his sermon, Reverend Wright was saying that if this country continues to play GOD and elevates itself above GOD with its policies on other nations, as with nations in the past according to the bible, GOD will not let that nation go unpunished and GOD will not bless that nation, but will damn that nation. So, when Reverend Wright said it's not GOD bless America, but GOD --damn America, Reverend Wright was not saying G.D. America as in one word and giving GOD a last name that HE does not have, but as in two words. For there was a pause between God and damn and television played it as one word. All he was saying was that this country is going to hell in a hand basket if it does not change its ways and turn back to GOD. In addition, it's hard for me to believe that this country ever did believe in GOD as it claims. Most of White America didn't even take the time to listen to his whole sermon, for if they did, they would have known that he was speaking the truth about America. And this country is not so great that it cannot be talked about by its citizens and if that makes a person unpatriotic, so be it. But television selected to demonize him and anyone else who dare to speak out against this country and its policies. Why is it that when a person who speaks out against America, who has served in America's armed forces such as the Reverend Jeremiah Wright has done is labeled as not being patriotic? But to the ignorance of some White folks and a few Blacks, it is because we live in a country where we can speak out against its policies that makes us patriots. In addition, Black folks were patriots long before they were citizens in this country. The late Dr.King said that it's not the words of our enemies that we will remember, but the silence of our friends who stood idly by and said nothing. I found nothing wrong with the statements made by Reverend Wright and in my opinion; it was out of his love that he have for this country to why he would make such statements. There's nothing more patriotic than for a man or woman to take a stand when they see their country wrong and voice their views on those wrongs and some White folks do not want the world to know the history of this country and all its evil doings it has inflicted on its citizens, especially the Black man. The Charlie Caucasians of this country are quick to label folks like Reverend Wright as the angry black man when they choose to speak out against this government and its above GOD policies. The white media do not want the world to see the White man as not being GOD or not being the face of GOD, but will do all it can to show the Black man as evil or the representation of evil. Now, some of you may not believe this truth when I say that the White man wants the world to see him as the face of GOD and/or to have some of us not to think that he is not GOD. But here is my proof. Throughout millions of homes and churches in this country and around the world, what is the complexion of the man to whom this country say is Jesus? He is White in complexion and many Black folks in this country have had and some continue to have a painted portrait of a White man depicted as Jesus hanging on the walls of their homes, sitting on some table or nightstand for a great number of years. Black preachers have pointed to this portrait in their churches for years when they preach their sermons. Grandpa and grandma have prayed to this portrait for years and if you are honest with yourself, you may have prayed to this sandy haired, bearded chin, blue-eyed Caucasian also. But, here's the kicker, not one person within the last two thousand plus years that is breathing heaven's air has ever seen Jesus, but yet, Mr. Charlie has made Him out to be a White man since the very day he planted his foot on this land after he stole it from the Indians and said, honey, I'm home. Once again, as I have stated earlier in chapter one, this is a calculated strategy of cultural conditioning. And do not think for one second that Mr. Charlie do not take this depiction of Jesus serious, for if you think back to just a few years ago if I'm not mistaken, a young kid in elementary school painted a portrait of a black Jesus and Mr. Charlie or in this case, the school system, went off because of this black portrait of Jesus. For they did not want the world to see the son of GOD if you believe in the bible as I do that says that's who Jesus is as anyone else other than a White man. Television did the same to First Lady Michele Obama as they did with Reverend Wright when she made the statement that for the first time in her adult life, she was REALLY PROUD of this country by nominating a Black man for President of the United States of America. The white media took out the word REALLY and played it across the airwaves that she said for the FIRST time in her adult life she is proud of this country. As you can see, by taking out the word REALLY, the white media changed her whole statement and gave it a different meaning and made First-Lady Michele Obama look as if this country has never done anything at all that she could be proud of until the nomination of her husband Senator Obama at the time as Presidential Candidate Obama and all those so called respectable news anchors knew this, but chose not to correct it, because as I said before, the white media want the world to see the White man as GOD or the face of GOD, but see the Black man and the Black woman as evil or the representation of evil. And then some of us black folks want to put all of our trust in the White man news media and chose to believe the very false report that they aired about Reverend Wright and First Lady Michelle Obama. But hey, who am I to say something about his people? Let me make it very clear once again, this book is not to demonize all White people or to make it seem that all White people are bad because that wouldn't be a true statement. As I said before and I do so again, there are plenty of goodhearted, non-racist, non- prejudice White people out there that love and care for people just because they are part of the human race, for there are bad and evil folks in every nation of people and Charlie Caucasian is just a very small minority among a whole and I hope that we are clear on that. Television also plays a huge part in the lives of our children. With today's cable and satellite providers, our children are indoctrinated by its images both day and night, 24 hours a day, 7 days a week, good, bad and worst alike. With cable; satellite and the internet, kids are spending more time watching their favorite TV shows like BET, which in my opinion stands for BLACKS EMBRASSEING THEMSELVES, to VH 1, to all kinds of reality shows like, For the love of Ray J., to the Favor of love and many others. Kids have a never-ending supply of programs that they can watch and kids are being raised by the television, for the television is training our kids on how to conduct themselves to the language they now speak, even to the way young men's wear their clothes. I want to take the time to say this before I move on since I'm on language and hopefully it will give you a new perspective when it comes to our language, than I will give my take on the slack down pants. You being a black man, why would you want to call another black man a Nigger or Nigga? I look at it like this, my grandparents were born in the early 1900's, my father was born in 1925 and my mother was born in 1936. Now, me knowing a little bit about the history of racism in this country and my parents and grandparents along with perhaps your parents and grandparents were born in a time that they were called Nigger by the White man to degrade them, to demean them and to dehumanize them, than why would you and I choose to disrespect, dishonor and shame their memory by calling one another the very term that Mr. Charlie has labeled our ancestors and parents as. And when we say this, we laugh, smile and joke about it. However, I want you to think about it this way the next time you call another black man or young person Nigger or Nigga. Someone in your family lost their life behind that word so that you wouldn't live as a Nigger or Nigga, or be called that by the White man and live out his meaning of the word that he has designated you to being. Does it matter to you that they gave up their life and many had their lives' taken not knowing that you would someday call one another the very word that was branded in their skin as they were burned to death? Why in the hell would I want to call you a word that was painted across some sign that was nailed over the head of a black man as the KKK lynched him by the neck as live escaped his broken body. If you think that that word is a word that we can make fun of, than you should find the mother of the young Emmitt Teal and tell her, that it was no big deal that a lynch mob murdered her son as he was being called the very word that many of us say without shame. I'm pretty sure she will welcome your explanation for calling another black person that with open arms and a smile while she offer you a slice of apple pie and a glass of Kool-aid. Surely those folks in your family who lost their lives' musta had some idea that you would someday value their sacrifice as worthless, than why else would they have fought so hard not to be the very word that you call each other? Once again, does it matter to you that they gave up their life and many had their lives' taken not knowing that you would someday call one another the very word that was painted on their mutilated body for all to see as their corpse hung from a tree? Surely, they musta had some idea that you would someday value their sacrifice as worthless, than why else would they have fought so hard not to be the very word that you call each other? And yes, it was worth repeating. Surely the young fourteen year old Emmitt Teal who was taken from his relatives home late one night by Charlie Caucasian and his Klansmen because it was said that he whistle at a White lady and was savagely beaten beyond recognition, his body thrown in a river, called NIGGER as he was being brutalized, surely he musta had some idea that you would be calling one another this word as something to be proud of. And to think that these courageous black people gave up their lives' just so that you can take pleasure in calling another man or boy, NIGGER or NIGGA. How foolish of them to have thought that someday we wouldn't be calling each other "NIGGER" or "NIGGA". And I will say again, how foolish of them to think. I hope that this will give you something to think about. I encourage you to visit the web site (www.awarforyoursoul.com) to gain a better understanding of the word "NIGGER or NIGGA" And some may wander to why I ask the question, So, what's wrong Black man? Television also influences our black kids not only in the language they speak ,but also on the way they dress and I would like to give my take on slack down pants which in my opinion is down right discussing. Not only are young blacks wearing their pants well down below their waist, but the trend has been adopted by other ethic groups around the country. Rap music and television can take that credit. If you would ask young people where slack pants originated, more than half couldn't tell you, another portion will say videos and the other half would probably say jail or the chain gang. Once again, television are teaching our kids false history and I will educate you on the originality of the slack down pants, so here goes. Slack down pants didn't start in the videos, in the jailhouse or on some chain gang, but during slavery. Not every Mr. Charlie back then was straight as six o'clock but bent like 6:15, on the down low long before that guy wrote the book on it. You see, the master who was on the low would rape the Black females and then turn around and have some of his down low brothers to come over and rape the Black male in front of the Black female to show his dominance over the Black male. They would force slaves to have sex with them by breaking them into having sex and those who chose to fight against this act were often times beaten and sometimes killed. Those who was broken were identified by making them to wear there pants below their waist to show that they were broken and wouldn't put up a fight even if they were sold to other slave master's that may have been on the low. But once again, Mr. Charlie deliberately withhold this history from being broadcast across the airwaves, simply because as I have stated before, he does not want the outside world to know his true history and the evil doings which he has committed. Television has taken place of outdoor recreational activities and than we wander, why our kids are so out of shape and obese. Young people are learning more and more from the television set than they are from their teachers and parents. Just look around your very own neighborhood, how many kids do you see outside running, jumping and playing in the neighborhood? Years ago while I was growing up, you couldn't keep me, my cousins and my friends from playing ball well into the night no matter what the weather was like. My mom had to make me come in the house to eat dinner, but with today's kids, with that television, that X-box 360 and that Wii game, you have to burn the house down to get them out of it and God forbid if you tell them to go outside and play, they'll look at you as if you physically abused them by saying that and they have social service on speed dial when you tell them to go outside and play. We have to do as President Obama has said on many occasions; we have to turn off the video games, the computer, the internet and the TV. We have to get our black kids out from in front of the TV and not just the black kids, but all kids if WE expect them to compete with kids from other nations that will be creating the jobs of tomorrow. But, once again, Who am I to say something about his people? Television as with the education system in this country, has culturally conditioned the minds of Black men's all across this country and once again, we pass that same mind set on to our kids because our parents passed it on to us and the trend continues. Once again, I will make it plain, I'm not faulting or saying that all White men are bad, but what I am saying is that the POWERS TO BE have done a job on our black kids and the black community. And through their GREED and their lust for POWER, his own kind is being caught up by the images of Sex, Violence and Drugs that bombard us on television. He has laid out a trap for one kind of bird (The Black man) and through his appetite to gain more, other birds (White kids and others) has so carelessly wandered in his trap. Now, let's take another look at the wonderful world of the television and how the programming has changed down through the years as far as BLACK SHOWS are concern. When I was growing up, we watched a show called GOOD TIMES; it was about the EVANS family. A close nit black family that lived in the projects of Chicago. The father's name was James and the mother's name was Florida, a husband and wife team raising their three children. Yeah, they were poor and always struggling, but they had love, unity and pride. And they always struck together no matter what they faced. James the father, was that strong black male that took care of his family to the best of his ability and was always their for his kids, maybe not with money, but with encouragement, hope and love. He was the one that enforced the rules of the house and he stressed the important of education in his own unique way to his kids along with his wife. Mrs. Evans was the glue that held the family together, that strong black female that displayed the proud heritage of her people when it came down to her family. Now, If you were one of those kids who grow up watching the GOOD TIMES, you should have notice that J.J., THELMA and MICHAEL didn't watch a lot of television and I know some of you are going to say, they didn't watch a lot of television because it was probably broke and I'll give you that, but when it wasn't broke, you always saw them at the kitchen table with their books or you always saw J.J. painting, Michael studying and Thelma in the kitchen trying to learn how to cook. Let us go to another Black show called The Jefferson's. Here we have George and Louise Jefferson, the proud owners of Jefferson Dry Cleaners that is based in New York City. Now George Jefferson may not have been the smartest business man to run a business, but what the show showed us was that with hard work and determination, one who may have came up poor can rise to the top by not placing blame, fault and finding excuses for not making it. And it also gave us a sense of pride just seeing this loud mouth Black man, who made it in the White man's world and encouraged his son Lionel to do the same. On many occasions, George made his boast for making it, moving into a deluxe apartment in the sky and finally getting his piece of the White man's pie. There's nothing wrong with making your boast when you have made it and certainly George was not ashamed by it, but one thing he never forgot was where he came from. He never forgot his roots nor that he was a Black man. My last example is a show that showed us another side of the Black family, the professional side. THE COSBY SHOW. Cliff and Clara Huxable and their four children. Here you had a well to do family. One's a doctor and the other is a lawyer and they both were college graduates and successful in their respected fields; like millions of Americans throughout the eighties, we all fell in love with that black family and they pushed all their children towards college and once again, their kids didn't watch a lot of television, play video games or clowned around in school. They always stressed the importance of education just like our ancestors did back then and to where we need to do more of today. These shows showed us that even when you are

DECISIONS not MISTAKES or EXCUSES. The bible clearly states that **"What so ever a man sow, so shall he also reap."** Good choices/decisions reap rewards. Bad choices/decisions reap consequences. Now I know that some of these things written in this book may have you a little upset with White people and that's a natural emotion, but this book is not written to hate White people, but rather grow beyond Mr. Charlie's opinion of you. It is to open your wonderful mind and have you look within yourself and see that you are more than what is shown of you on television. To a degree, we shouldn't be mad at the White man, for he is doing what he is programmed to do and we can't continue to blame him for our down falls, and short comings. However, If I'm going to keep it real, than I will keep it real. The ones to whom we should be angry at are those simple minded, lazy, good for nothing Negros who continue to let their lives be the reality of the evil slave master's of old. Television has made it so that the Black man is seen as the most despicable human being in this country. When a black youth is walking around in the mall, they are scrutinized more so than any other race of people. White women cling to their purses and walk with an element of fear when they are within the vicinity of black youths. Television has made it so that the view of the Black man is only that of violence and chaos. It has brainwashed other ethnic groups in this country and around the world that because of our skin color, we are cursed by GOD and we are the representation of evil. The Reverend Pat Robertson of the famous 700 club made an idiotic statement during the Haiti earthquake that GOD is punishing the Haitian people because they made a pact with the devil when they fought to be free and through this so-called pact, they were able to conquer the White French. Once again, Charlie Caucasian (Pat Robertson) is depicting (Joe Johnson) the Black man as the representation of evil. But yet, Mr. Charlie said nothing when 9/11 happened. The only statements you heard from folks like Pat Robertson is how evil those 911 hi-jackers were for attacking this great nation of his and if you had paid close attention to what you are reading, what Charlie Caucasian was really saying was this, how dare those people attack GOD. Like I say, Mr. Charlie shows himself as GOD or the face of GOD and there is no difference between him and America, for America is a manifestation of him and television is his source to portray such an image throughout the world. As a whole, television does not show that WE are caring and loving fathers, faithful

struggling, you can still band together as a unit and keep your di
about yourself as we see in GOODTIMES. These shows showed u
with hard work and not becoming the reality of your surrounding:
too can make it out of the projects and become a successful bu:
person as we see in THE Jefferson's. And these shows showed u:
the family unit that consists of a husband and a wife who made a so
commitment to be that positive influence in their children lives'
one element that we shouldn't allow to escape the Black family ar
see that in The Cosby Show. These were three wholesome shows
although the families were in different positions in life, televisior
little to do with their children thinking and the shapening of
minds. In today's television, you don't see wholesome black fa
shows anymore where there is a husband and wife or a sense of l
pride and dignity, but now what you see as far as the black family l
portrayed on television is a single mom raising her child while the f:
is in jail or worst, dead from a drug sell gone bad. Black family sl
are in a comedic setting most of the time on television and some
wander to why they take us as a joke. B.E.T. has gone as far as sho·
the Black family in a cartoon setting like THE BOONDOCKS, w
is a total disgrace to the Black race with all its NIGGER (N
WHORES and B calling. It portrays the Black young in a negative
with gang violence, drug activity, robbing and stealing, sex and sc
dropout. Take Denzel in the movie Training Day. It took a role
dirty cop for him to win an Oscar and was barely mention whe
played Malcolm X. The beautiful Halle Berry did not win an Osca
her role as the legendary jazz singer Dorthory Dandridge, but wo
her role in Monster Ball where she had a nude screen. Monique'
an Oscar portraying a role as a very abusive, foul mouthing moth
the movie Precious. But how can we get mad at the producers of :
shows when we live out that reality each and every day when we fir
the television and see the six o'clock news hauling off our young
and women in the back of a policemen's car or we see another sens
killing that should never have taken place or we see the destruction
we are causing within our own community and teen pregnancy on
rise and parents finding a legitimate excuse for it by telling their yo
daughters that they made a mistake instead of telling them that
made a bad decision and the result of their actions is motherhood.
need to start telling our kids that life is based on CHOICES

DECISIONS not MISTAKES or EXCUSES. The bible clearly states that **"What so ever a man sow, so shall he also reap."** Good choices/decisions reap rewards. Bad choices/decisions reap consequences. Now I know that some of these things written in this book may have you a little upset with White people and that's a natural emotion, but this book is not written to hate White people, but rather grow beyond Mr. Charlie's opinion of you. It is to open your wonderful mind and have you look within yourself and see that you are more than what is shown of you on television. To a degree, we shouldn't be mad at the White man, for he is doing what he is programmed to do and we can't continue to blame him for our down falls, and short comings. However, If I'm going to keep it real, than I will keep it real. The ones to whom we should be angry at are those simple minded, lazy, good for nothing Negros who continue to let their lives be the reality of the evil slave master's of old. Television has made it so that the Black man is seen as the most despicable human being in this country. When a black youth is walking around in the mall, they are scrutinized more so than any other race of people. White women cling to their purses and walk with an element of fear when they are within the vicinity of black youths. Television has made it so that the view of the Black man is only that of violence and chaos. It has brainwashed other ethnic groups in this country and around the world that because of our skin color, we are cursed by GOD and we are the representation of evil. The Reverend Pat Robertson of the famous 700 club made an idiotic statement during the Haiti earthquake that GOD is punishing the Haitian people because they made a pact with the devil when they fought to be free and through this so-called pact, they were able to conquer the White French. Once again, Charlie Caucasian (Pat Robertson) is depicting (Joe Johnson) the Black man as the representation of evil. But yet, Mr. Charlie said nothing when 9/11 happened. The only statements you heard from folks like Pat Robertson is how evil those 911 hi-jackers were for attacking this great nation of his and if you had paid close attention to what you are reading, what Charlie Caucasian was really saying was this, how dare those people attack GOD. Like I say, Mr. Charlie shows himself as GOD or the face of GOD and there is no difference between him and America, for America is a manifestation of him and television is his source to portray such an image throughout the world. As a whole, television does not show that WE are caring and loving fathers, faithful struggling, you can still band together as a unit and keep your dignity about yourself as we see in GOODTIMES. These shows showed us that with hard work and not becoming the reality of your surroundings, you too can make it out of the projects and become a successful business person as we see in THE Jefferson's. And these shows showed us that the family unit that consists of a husband and a wife who made a solemn commitment to be that positive influence in their children lives' is the one element that we shouldn't allow to escape the Black family and we see that in The Cosby Show. These were three wholesome shows that although the families were in different positions in life, television had little to do with their children thinking and the shapening of their minds. In today's television, you don't see wholesome black family shows anymore where there is a husband and wife or a sense of black pride and dignity, but now what you see as far as the black family being portrayed on television is a single mom raising her child while the father is in jail or worst, dead from a drug sell gone bad. Black family shows are in a comedic setting most of the time on television and some may wander to why they take us as a joke. B.E.T. has gone as far as showing the Black family in a cartoon setting like THE BOONDOCKS, which is a total disgrace to the Black race with all its NIGGER (Nigga) WHORES and B calling. It portrays the Black young in a negative light with gang violence, drug activity, robbing and stealing, sex and school dropout. Take Denzel in the movie Training Day. It took a role of a dirty cop for him to win an Oscar and was barely mention when he played Malcolm X. The beautiful Halle Berry did not win an Oscar for her role as the legendary jazz singer Dorthory Dandridge, but won for her role in Monster Ball where she had a nude screen. Monique' won an Oscar portraying a role as a very abusive, foul mouthing mother in the movie Precious. But how can we get mad at the producers of such shows when we live out that reality each and every day when we fire up the television and see the six o'clock news hauling off our young men and women in the back of a policemen's car or we see another senseless killing that should never have taken place or we see the destruction that we are causing within our own community and teen pregnancy on the rise and parents finding a legitimate excuse for it by telling their young daughters that they made a mistake instead of telling them that they made a bad decision and the result of their actions is motherhood. We need to start telling our kids that life is based on CHOICES and

and committed husbands, good sons and daughters, great leaders in the community and a people who loved and fought for this country even when this country didn't love and fight for us, but hated us with a passion and fought to keep us as nothing more than a NIGGER. And to think that I would want to give such bigotry and hatred a platform to stand on and the satisfaction of fulfilling the slave master's view of me by calling one of my black brother's a NIGGER or NIGGA and my black sister a B**** or a WHORE. But once again, who am I to say something about his people? Television make it seems OK to drop-out of school or to have sex with a various number of partners. And with videos showing girls shaking their assets and showing off their bodies, television has influenced young girls into thinking that it's perfectly find to sell their body and their dignity if they want to get ahead. It seems that our young girls these days have no shame in their actions anymore or how they are viewed by them. They are in school making packs on who can get pregnant the fastest or who can sleep with the most guys in a year's time. A big part of the problem with this teen pregnancy epidemic is that parents no longer have time for their kids and their kids are out there having unprotected sex with anyone that is not related to them. Parents are becoming more and more younger in today's society and what was once unacceptable in our community is now acceptable and a lot of that stems from the images that they see on television. When I was growing up, it would pain me to my heart if I did something that I know my parents wouldn't approve of and I wouldn't dare lie to my parents even if it meant getting my behind busted, but if you take a hard look at the actions of some of our girls today, they act more thuggish than some guys you and I may know with the language to match. Another huge part of our problem is how television depicts our young girls as hoochi mama's when it comes down to teen-age respectability. It tells our girls that in order to feel beautiful and sexy you must show as much skin as you possibly can without breaking the law. Years ago in the black community, you couldn't pay a black mother enough money in a sense to dress her little girl up in a mini skirt this was well above her little knee caps, but look at the fashion of today for little girl's. They have mini skirts; short cut blouses and shirts; skin tight jeans that are so tight that it looks as if they were painted on with a spray gun. It has even gotten to the point that they have high heel shoes that has been scaled down to their size followed up by little make up kits. Six and seven year olds don't want long dresses anymore because their teen age parent is not mature enough to know any difference and their parent thought it was so cute when they dressed their child up as if they were an adult. And than we wander why our kids are going astray, becoming sexually active before they reach the age of twelve and curse us out by age thirteen. But, Who am I to say something about my people? Here's a statement that may put some of you women in a little uproar, and once again I will say if it does, so be it, for I will not attempt to find an excuse for telling the truth to my beautiful people, but hopefully supply you a reason to why I make such a statement. Back in the day, women would say that men are dogs and would classified them as such, but if you look at how some of these young girls and some of these older women are conducting themselves, they are doing their share of barking also and by doing their share of barking, boy's who consider themselves men call women out of their name based on the actions they display out in society and the images that is shown on television is their proof that this is an acceptable reaction to what should be an unacceptable reality. It has gotten to the point that black girls call each other B****, and laugh afterwards. Look at rapper Lil'Kim, she call herself the QUEEN B. And because of the position that she's in and the influence she has, young girls who desire to be like her have it in their young minds that it must be OK to be called a B**** or a Whore and say to themselves, if someone like Lil' Kim can call herself that, than it must be OK. And if you look at our young men, when they hear girls calling themselves WHORE'S and B's, than why wouldn't they do the same, for they look at it as, if you care nothing for calling yourself that or having no shame about it, than why should I? Young men's are quick to say that I'm calling you what you call yourself. Here is a simple statement that black men can make to these young boys and hopefully bring a positive change in their view of black girls and realize that they are a product of that woman to whom they are calling out of there name. I look at it this way and some of you who are reading this book may not see it like I do and that's perfectly fine, but why would I want to call any woman a B**** when I had a mother. Why would I want to call a woman a B**** when I have sisters and why would I want to call a woman a B**** when I have two daughters and two young granddaughters myself. So, why would you want to call the vehicle that GOD chose to birth you into this world a B****, but hey, you may be a test tube baby and if so, than I guess you think you have a legitimate reason for doing so, but once again, it takes a woman's egg to perform that. I tell young boys this here, if you think that it is OK to call a woman B****, then go home and call your mom or your grandmother a Whore or a B**** and let me know what day you wake up after they have knocked you the hell out. If you choose not to call your own mother or grandmother this, do not call someone else's, because if you are going to keep it real by calling one woman this degrading name, than call ALL women this degrading name including your own mother or grandmother. Black men need to tell these young boys if you would not call your mom or your grandma out of there name, than you shouldn't want to call another woman that and if you do, than you shouldn't get mad at someone else if they say that about your mom or grandma. Then again, a lot of us do not correct our own kids. So correcting someone else's child is out of the question, for many black men have grown spineless. And I will say again, television have a lot to do with how black youth view one another. Some studies show that kids spend up to 8-12 hours per night looking at various shows on television once they get home from school and even longer on the weekend and some parents continue to see this as not being a problem. But once again, Who am I too say something about his people? And than some may wander to why I ask the question, So, what's wrong Black man? And the answer is, ME.

Ch. 3 - Radio and Music:
How it is shapening our kids

Now, let's move to the music world. Music is one of the most powerful forces in this country. It has transcended race, broke down walls and built bridges all across this planet. It perhaps has more of an influence on our young people today than that of the television. However, look at how music has changed down through the years. Back in the day, we had artistes that were not afraid to sing about all the wrongs and all the injustices that were going on in this country. Music was put out there according to the condition of not only black America, but the country itself. In my opinion, artistes back then had a backbone, a soul and a conscience. It have gone from musicians like James Brown who sang about the drug Heroin that was infesting the black neighborhood (King Heroin) and the devastating effect it could have on one's life to Marvin Gale who sang a song called (Mercy Mercy me) to Michael Jackson with his song named (A Man in the Mirror) There is a line in that Michael Jackson song that is so prevalent for today's times and it goes like this: **"I'm struggling with the man in the mirror, I'm asking him to change his way's, no message can any clearer, so if you want to make the world a better place you have to look at yourself and make a CHANGE".** As what Mike is singing about, he is telling us that if we want to change the world and make it a better place for us ALL, we need to ask the person within ourselves to change his ways, see the world from another advantage point, and help those who may be less fortunate. I'm just a strong believer in that WE shouldn't put material things before our follow man as many of our artistes do today by the selling of their soul and their conscience. And it will take this kind of thinking to make this world and this above GOD country a better place. Black families in the day would listen to songs with a vibrate joy within their heart. Songs that would inspire, inform, renew and encourage a people and let them know that the possibility of things getting better was possible despite their current situation and condition. Artist like Harold Melvin and the Blue Notes featuring Teddy Pendergrass who sang a song called, WAKE UP EVERYBODY, which addressed the education and economic problems in this country along with War, Hatred, Laziness and Poverty. Here's a line that we all need to take heed of. It went a little like this : **"Wake up everybody, no more sleeping in bed, no more backward thinking, time for thinking ahead, the world has changed so very much, from where it use to be. The World is filled with hatred, war and poverty. Wake up all the teachers, time to teach a new way, maybe than they'll listen, to what you have to say. They're the ones who's coming up and the world is in their hands, teach all the children, teach them the very best you can. The world will get no better, if we just let it be. We have to change the world for you and me".** Teddy was telling us through song that we can no longer sit back and expect our change to come without putting forth an effort of sacrifice to bring about the change that we so desperate needed. And I have to believe that this song was not only for the Black community, but the nation as a whole. Songs like this touch the core of one's soul when the words flowed through the speakers of your stereo. Once again, I will say, most artist back in the day cared about the state of the Black community and they had a conscience about the music they put out. Now, look at the artist of today for they have no conscience about the music they put out, nor do their music if you can call it that have the uplifting power that music had back then. Music that could uplift a generation and propel them to move forward. Songs that said that whatever you were going through, there is something much bigger than you. There was music that empowered a people to march forward even after being beaten by evil white's during the Selma march. Songs like WE SHALL OVERCOME and I'M NOT GOING TO LET NOTHING TURN ME AROUND. These songs inspired a people and moved a nation towards equality and justice. But those types of songs are long forgotten, because if you're not cursing, fighting and spiting out the "N" word or the "B" word, than some of these black owned record label do not want to hear your rap. And no matter how much some of us to a degree dislike rap music, it is the biggest influence in our kids lives today. I do believe that some of this rap music is crippling our young people because they want to be the next Jay-Z or Fifty cent. And some of you may say why would I write such a thing and I'm glad you ask. I say this because many of our young people can remember a rap song that they heard just once, but can't read a third grade English book or remember to do their homework. Than some may wander to why I ask the question, So, what's wrong Black man? If you do not have an answer to this question thus far, keep reading. Rappers back in the day like Dana Dane took the Cinderella story and turned it into a rap song (Cindafello) about a young black boy who would be crowned king as Cinderella was crowned queen in the story. You had KRS-1 who rapped about education with a rap song called (You must learn.) that stress the importance of education and their was the group Public Enemy who rapped about the problems that plagued the black youth with the rap song (Self-destruction) Years ago record companies wouldn't dare let an artist say the word's B**** or Nigger in a song, but now, rap artists can't make a record without calling the women that bought them into the world a B**** and can't uplift the Black man because he is calling him Nigger or a Nigga. White executives have lifted the band of such words because they have come to realize that black boys of this generation have no self-respect for themselves or their people. The White man have figured out that if he let Black rappers say those types of words in their songs, play them across the air waves, than he would surely degrade and demean his race down to the level of some flea infested dog and he will do it with a smile on his face and a pay check in his hand, being that materialistic slave for the White man. They have become so ignorant in their understanding of self, their history and the struggle, that the White man can now sit back on the porch with his legs crossed, along with Charlie Caucasian at his side, a Pat's Blue Ribbon beer in his hand, a cigar in his mouth, a confederate flag hanging over his doorway and say, You see Charlie, I told you that if we let those Black niggers, oh, I mean, Black boys say those kinds of words, I told you that they will call each other's mom and grandma a B**** and their father and grandfather a Nigger or Nigga. Charlie, I told you that Black people will accept anything that we throw them like a dog sitting at the table waiting for a bone and will be happier than a run away slave with papers on broad the freedom train if we lift the band of such words. Charlie, I rather see a black nigger girl or I mean, nigga girl, as the rappers say, shaking her tail feather in a rap video and calling herself QUEEN B**** than to have her sitting in some college professor's classroom learning about science, mathematics, history, bio-tech, computers and what have you. And that way it will be one less affirmative action Black B**** my daughter or granddaughter would have to complete with to get a job. Now I'm not saying that all White people think and talk this way, only a small minority and some folks just not going to change even if Jesus Himself come down from Heaven and tell them to their face that their way of thinking is wrong. And the radio that plays this type of junk isn't helping either, for they have changed also. James Brown and Stevie Wonder was buying radio stations back then and they were not even close to making the money that these so called artist are today, but once again, they had a conscience when it came to the state of the Black man and during that time, the radio was the only source of information that the black community had to rely on. Music and radio back then in my opinion was worth more than a paycheck, it was worth a people. But once again, Who am I to say something about his people? As we can see, music and radio has shaped the minds of our kids and our culture to the effect that we as a people do not value our own race. In addition, our black youths through the influence that music, radio and rappers have on them have chosen to emulate that in which they hear and see. Video has made it glamorous to be a thug and being shot is equivalent to the Purple Heart that one receives on the battlefield for bravery. Music, radio and videos has transformed our young people minds so that if you ask a young child what he or she hope to be when they get older, most will respond a high percentage of the time with answers somewhere in the neighborhood of a rapper, ball player or a video model of some sort. Our kids no longer dream of being doctor's, lawyer's, engineers, scientist or a company CEO or president. These are not as glamorous as seeing a carload of beautiful girls in a Bentley with a fist full of money drinking Cristal. And one of the reason's for this thinking is that music video's make it seems that success comes in the form of money, drugs, cars ,girls, guns and all the material items one could ever hope to possess. Moreover, these rappers will not take responsibility for the contents that they put into their music videos nor do they see anything wrong because they themselves are puppets or in other words and to bring it closer to home, 2010 slaves. If we want to get the attention of some of these rappers and the record companies, stop buying this filth that is toxic to the black community and by doing so, maybe they will put some positive music out there that can get our black youth on a clearer path. When will we as Black men realize that we cannot afford to lose such a great human commodity, that being our youth. But once again, who am I to say something about his people? And some may wander to why I ask the question, So, What's wrong Black man? And the answer is: ME.

Ch. 4 - History:
How it changed who we are

Not only has cultural conditioning affected the Black man in television and education, but also in the area of our history. You remember the statement that I wrote on radio talk show host personality Joe Madison and what he said about cultural conditioning. That in this country, we are lead to believe that White is superior, Black is inferior and the manifestation of that cultural conditioning is that Black people are Undervalued, Underestimated and Marginalize. In my opinion, one of the reasons to why the Black man is in the state that he is in is that he has fail to value his history and he has passed that devaluing on to his kids. So, our black youths of today do not value the sacrifices of the past and by doing so, they jeopardize their future all because the older generation has fail them. We are a rich people in cultural and in heritage. But along the way, we have lost that connection that made us a people and we have chosen that which has become the White man's God for ourselves. And that is Money and Greed fueled by selfishness. Our history has been systematically distorted in such a way that we don't know who we are and we have become so much like Charlie Caucasian that we view one another as that flea infested dog. Our history has been striped from us and I believe that its purpose was so that we wouldn't find out that we were the Kings and Queens in the land of Africa. It was striped from us to keep us separate as a united people. You see, if the black man is kept from his history and not know that he is the descendent of royalty, then he will accept whatever is written about him as being true. Look at the history books that your kids are reading, they mostly only speak of the White man's history and a lot of that history is fabricated and once again, it is to make the White man to be God or to be the face of God. The history facts of the Negro man were deliberately distorted from the history books to systematically deprive the Negro child of their heritage and to reduce him or her to nothingness and nobodyness. For years it was written that the explorer Robert E. Peary was the first man to have made it successfully to the North Pole, but that turned out to be false. Matthew Henson is believed to be the very first man to have actually reached the North Pole, some forty-five minuets before Peary on April 6, 1909. But a Dr. Frederick Cook who had been with Peary and Henson on an earlier trip to Greenland told a bold face lie that, he himself had successfully reached the North Pole a full year before Henson and Peary on April 21st , 1908. Matthew Alexander Henson, a black man, was an assistant of Peary, journeyed on when Commander Robert E. Peary became frostbitten and could not go any further under his own strength but was pulled by Eskimos as Henson made a dash for the pole. There are conflicting dates as to the actual day, but nevertheless, a Black man was there. It wasn't until 1937, at age seventy, that Henson was recognized for what he had achieved and got the recognition he so rightly deserved. It was in that same year that Matthew Henson was made an honorary member of the famed Explorers Club in New York. In the year of 1946, he was honored by the U.S.Navy with a medal. Many folks that knew Henson said that his most heartfelt prize as spoken by him was a gold medal, which he received from the Chicago Geographic Society that honored his brave achievement. Henson died on March 9th, 1955, and was buried at the Woodlawn Cemetery in the Bronx. In 1987, a Dr.S. Allen Counter, the man who wrote the biography story of Henson's life, led a movement to have the remains of both Henson and his wife moved to lay adjacent to Robert Peary in Arlington National Cemetery. A place where some of our greatest hero's are remembered and immortalized. A fitting location for one of America's finest Black hero's. The late President Ronald Reagan granted permission during his Presidency and on the seventy-ninth anniversary of the discovery of the North Pole, Henson was laid to rest near his friend. History books were revised and they showed that a Black man was co- discoverer of the successful journey to the North Pole. On April 6,1909, a Black man truly stood on top of the world and his name is, Matthew Alexander Henson. Look at the history of (The Colony of Saint-Domingue) better known today as Haiti. That small ravaged country was once considered to be the richest colony in the West Indies and probably the richest colony in the history of the world. It had fertile soil and ideal climate that produced sugar, coffee, cocoa, indigo, tobacco, cotton, sisal as well as some fruits and vegetables for the motherland France. Haiti gained its freedom by defeating King Louis XVI and Queen Marie Antoinette in 1791 to 1803, to become the first freed Black country in the world through a slave revolt because they made up in their minds that they would no longer be slaves. Here's a little cultural conditioning lesson for you. Even during the slave revolt in Haiti, some free blacks called (Mulattoes) children of White Frenchmen and slave women joined the Whites to fight against their own people simply because they were more White than the White Frenchmen themselves. They held their noses up so high that they could peep in on heaven itself and looked down on those who skin color were a little darker than there's. They were well to do slaves that could own land and slaves themselves and often treated their slaves worst than the White Frenchmen master did and they mostly always wanted to draw distinct lines between them and the slaves. Funny, it seems that we have Mulattoes within our own community today, who would have thought that many of us who has come up would be doing the very same thing that the Mulattoes had done? And this so called great country of ours wouldn't even recognize Haiti as a country for some sixty plus years because of the Haiti revolt, along with other countries such as England and Spain. And yes, you read it correctly, I said this so called great country of ours because as with the late Dr. King have said, if this country want to live up to its greatness that it claims to be, it has to treat ALL its citizens with love, respect and equality. I'm not saying that this country has not done great things, because it has and it continue to stride towards greatness, but if I had to rate this America of ours, it would stop at GOOD. America is a GOOD country, but not a great country in my opinion. America has put Haiti under economic hardship by exploiting their people, land and resources. In addition to that, the reason behind such a position from the United States was that the United States governorment did not want what happen in Haiti's slave revolt to influence the slaves in this country and cause them to rise up and rebel against slave oppression. And what's more important than that in my opinion was not so much as a slave uprising, but the money that would be lost because for one. France lost billions of dollars because of the uprising of Haitian slaves. We can rise up and rebel today and I'm not talking about violence, but what I am talking about is that we can rebel by learning our history, getting educated, living up to the expectation that our ancestors fought and died for, respect one another and above all, LOVE ONE ANOTHER. Since the White man has given us a little bit of freedom in this country, we have gotten to the point that we care absolutely nothing for our history. The White man's history is well intact and our history is slowly becoming a faded memory, simply because a lot of us look at our history as something not to build on but something we hope to forget. As I have stated before, we have become materialistic slaves and most of us do not know it. I remember reading a statement on what Harriett Tubman said, the Black Moses of our people incase you didn't know. She said in an interview when a question was asked about how many slaves she led to freedom and she replied, hundreds, but I could have freed a lot more if only they had known they were slaves. As I have said, many of us today are slaves and don't even know it. How many of us know that Marcus Garvey was a businessman, a journalist, a Black Nationalist, an entrepreneur and he owned ships. He wanted Blacks to produce their own products and become self-sufficient by trading with the continent of Africa. But yet, we don't encourage our black youth to support their own kind, shame on us. We do not encourage our kids to think of themselves as business owners but rather business supporters. We encourage them to be the next Michael Jordan, but not the next Robert Johnson the owner of the Charlotte Bobcats. The first African-American to have owned a professional team that is now owned by Michael Jordan. We encourage them to go off to college and get a good education so that they may get a great job rather than to encourage them that once they graduate, rather than to only look to getting a job, create a job. Instead of becoming an employee, become an employer. This is a little quote from famous motivator speaker Les Brown, he says this (If you have a job, you are on a fixed income, if you think that you are not, than give yourself a raise tomorrow) This is such a powerful quote and all it is saying is that you are limited by your job and your income is bonded to that 9 to 5. We have become so jealous over one another that its down right sickening. And this is what I mean. There are two stores, one owned by a Black man in the black neighborhood and the other owned by a Asian American some ten miles away just outside the black community. Let's say that both stores sell hair care products, but the Black man must sell his products for fifty cents higher than the Asian man because the Asian community has the black hair market on lock and sisters will travel those ten miles just to save fifty cents, while burning up five dollars in gas than to buy that same hair care product from the Black man's store, whose product is fifty cents higher. And the first thing that we'll say out of our mouth is this: He'll not buy a Cadillac with my money and this is the attitude that we carry around. But here's the thing, they won't buy Mr. Jones product and there's a better chance that Mr. Jones will stop and help them if they are stranded along side the hi-way with a flat tire or something and will perhaps have a greater chance that Mr. Jones will invite them to dinner or buy them something to eat if they become hungry. But flip the coin, Mr. Chin care nothing for them except that they come in and spend their money in his store and will perhaps pass them by if they are stranded and don't even think that he will invite you to dinner. And if Mr. Chin ever need help in his store, who do you think he'll hire, surely not one of his biggest black customers nor will he spend any of his money in their black community. But because some of us can't see ourselves doing anything constructive, or to lazy to try, than we want to knock those of us who dare to dream that they will be the next Oprah, the next Robert Johnson, the next Michael Jordan , Russell Simons, General Colin Powell, Condoleezza Rice and whoever else a person gain inspiration from. However, this stems from not knowing that folks like Marcus Garvey who had a vision for his people and saw them as producers and not just consumers. Madam C.J.Walker, the Oprah Winfrey of her day who became the first Black female millionaire who made her fortune from the selling of hair care products. Walker, a Black woman who had the foresight to open her own bank and it still exists today. Most of us do not know that there once was a Black Wall Street in Tulsa, Oklahoma. One of the most affluent Black communities in all America. A community of wealthy blacks that spanned some 36 square blocks of profitable black businesses in the district of Northern Tulsa. There were over 600 successful black businesses. Among those businesses were 21 churches, 30 grocery stores, 2 movie theaters, 21 restaurants, a hospital, a bank, a post office, libraries, schools, law offices, a half dozen private planes and a bus system that was owned by a black doctor named, Dr.Berry. Black Wall Street was like a mini Beverly Hills before it was destroyed on June 1, 1921 by an onslaught of air bombs and burned to the ground by some envious white people. It took less than 12 hours and after the smoke cleared, some 3000 Africa Americans were dead and over 600 black businesses lost. Of course, as you may have guess, the infamous Ku Klux Klan was behind it all along with some high-ranking officials. All because Charlie Caucasian couldn't stand to see this thriving black community making it on their owns and the evil in his heart was demonstrated and carried out by the work of his evil hand. But once again, the White man do not want the outside world to know his evil history and it is not written in his history books and he wouldn't dare to speak on this horrible tragedy simply because he want to show himself as God or the face of God for all the world to see. He cannot stand it when his evil history is known beyond his borders by other nations and he is not viewed as the holy one of God, but the atrocious revelation of evil. He is committed to hide the truth about the atrocity methods that he had subjected the Black man and other people of color to as he established himself as the supreme ruler of earth, to a degree, more than God. However, let me say this again before some of you who are reading this section blow a gasket because of some of the statements made in this book. There are thousands of good hearted White folks in this country that follow the commandment that Jesus himself said, **(Treat others as you would have them to treat you)** and by that, many lost their lives doing the civil rights movement. Most of us do not know that the greatest squadron of fighter pilots was not the famous Blue Angels, or some other airborne brigade, but the Tuskegee Airmen. They were the 332nd fighter group of 1941. They flew some 200-escort missions that were under the command of the nation's first Black General, Benjamin O. Davis Jr. These men, despite the odds against them never lost one aircraft to enemy fire, a record unmatched by any other fighter group in military history and they were BLACK. It was the Black man in Africa that wore the gold and silver. Moreover, the Black woman wore the fine linen and the headdress. The Black man built the pyramids of Egypt, it was a Black man who planned Washington D.C., and it was Black slaves who built the White house. All I'm saying is that we came from intelligent people and we need to allow that evidence to show. We need to build on the foundation that was laid for us, not erase it. Let us make black history as we stride to preserve the history that was made. But, who am I to say something about his people? And than some may wander to why I ask the question So, what's wrong Black man? And the answer is, ME.

Ch. 5 - Economics:
A planned hardship

I will let you know now that I am no economic expert or some CPA sitting behind some fancy desk pushing out numbers, but what I am is a person who has seen and experienced the hardship of not educating himself on money and the responsibility of understanding it. You see, most black families know absolute nothing when it comes down to money and finance other than to spend every dime that they bring home out of every nine-cent check they make. And those of us who have obtained that knowledge and understanding are sometimes to stuck up on ourselves to share that knowledge with others so that the Black community as a whole would be more knowledgeable in that area. In addition to that statement, it is hardly ever talked about at the dinner table, probably because it is a subject that few black folks know anything about and we are to proud to admit it. As a whole, we look at money and finance as unimportant, not knowing that our kids are poorer now in the education of money than they were in the 1960's. Back in the day, Black men were more into saving their earnings than they are today. Maybe not so much in the sense of money per-say, but in the sense of stretching what they obtain to the next day and even the day after. We must develop this same mind set today, as it was yesterday if we are to build generational wealth for our kids and grandkids. I believe that Black men back then studied the way of the ant as the bible speaks of, in that the ant gathers his food in the summer in preparation for the winter. In other words, he is preparing for his future, he do not sit around and wait for the weather to get bad before he prepare for his future survival. He gets out there and makes it happen, unlike so many of us in the black community today who sit around and wait for GOD or the government to drop something in our laps. Talk show host and motivational speaker Willie Jolley has this saying that goes, **"If you are waiting for GOD to drop something in your lap, than you better get off your behind and move your lap to where GOD is dropping something."** Once again my brother, in other words, stop talking about being a millionaire, or that financial blessing, and put together a plan and make it happen. To be totally honest, most of our prepared future is what we have in our wallets and purses at the time and we to a degree give no thought to our future or the future of kids and this need to change. So, let's take an open look at how not knowing about money will leave us destitute in the future. In my opinion, I think that economic hardship was a planned effort by Charlie Caucasian to continue the miseducation of the black man. That by keeping him ignorant on finance, he will pass that reality on to his kids, because you can only pass on that which you know and if you do not cultivate your mind on money and finance, than how can you expect to grow? Once the Black man gained his freedom, the White man had to come up with a plan to keep him imprisoned, maybe not in body, but in his thinking through accruing debt that he could not pay. In addition to that, by not allowing him to go to school to be taught how to add, subtract, multiply, divide and read, thus causing him to mis-manage the money he or she did earn. Through cultural conditioning, the black man has been condition down through the years to consume rather than produce, and by nurturing and cultivating his need to obtain "THINGS" that has no lasting value; he has evolved in what I call a "Materialistic Slave". A materialistic slave is someone who will work all their life just to obtain THINGS or to have more than the next man or woman. They think that these THINGS will bring them peace and joy or fill that void in their lives'. Than when that flame goes out, than they hope to get that next spark with the next THING and it's a continuous roller coaster. The White man now know that he have a slave for life to buy his product and produce nothing but debt. That's one thing about us black people, we want "THINGS" even if we cannot afford them. I want it all is the black man motto and I will do whatever it takes to get it. For this is our way of thinking. It is more important for us to obtain "THINGS", than it is for us to obtain the knowledge about the thing that will better serve us in obtaining those "THINGS", that being money and finance. There's an old saying that goes; "He who die to obtain many things still dies." Black man, do not live the rest of your life just to obtain "THINGS" or do any and everything under heaven's sun just to have them, for I believe that you are better than some "Materialistic Slave" for Mr. Charlie. Because no matter how long you live to obtain those "THINGS", you still going to die and the only thing that folks will say about you is this: He or she sure had a lot of things. In addition, if it were possible for you to see what became of your "THINGS," they would probably be sold to bury you, simply because you were more into cars, jewelry, rims, music stereos and clothes that you forgot to purchase life insurance. Life insurance is another way for us to pass down generational wealth, for Mr. Charlie has been doing this for years, but hey, you want "THINGS," right. There's an old Hungarian proverb that goes like this: "It's not getting all that you want, but wanting all that you get." All it is saying is this, it shouldn't be so important to you to get all the "THINGS" you want in life, but wanting all those "THINGS" that will come to you in life. Oh yeah, "THINGS" are going to come in this life and the Nobel peace prize question is this, Do I want the "THINGS" that will come to me in life? Another way for us to build generational wealth is for us to swallow our pride and live below our means. Now I know what some of you may be saying or thinking right about now, what does he mean by living below my means? All I'm saying is this, If you work on a job and you bring home $500 per week, but you live on $501 per week, than how in the hell can you expect to build generational wealth or better yet, how in the hell do you expect to save money when you are living above that which you earn and for a lot of us, this is our reality. Now, turn this example around and you are now a person who has grown in the knowledge and understanding of money and finance and you bring home that same $500 per week, but you live off of $350 per week, that mean that you now have money to invest or save and you are on your way to building wealth and this is the reality that "WE" need to get too. Wealth comes in many forms, there's financial wealth, spiritual wealth, physical wealth, relationship wealth and wealth in knowledge and understanding, but I'm talking about money and financial wealth. Another thing that we in the black community need to do in my opinion is to invest and open up a bank account in a black owned bank. This is another way for us to build generational wealth, and by putting our money in banks that best represent us, it will show Mr. Charlie that we can target our money and he will see that we are a force to be reckon with and those very banks have a solid record of reinvesting back in our community unlike many banks that many of us bank with today. There are many black owned banks out there and if you care to look into them you can visit (www.blackownedbanks. com) for a list. Money is one of the most important subjects that we can learn about, but yet most high schools do not teach on the subject nor do they have a curriculum for it. In addition, by the time we do find out about the importance of money and finance if ever, we are thousands of dollars in debt. But not let us get to far ahead of ourselves, for this finance mis-education of the Black man as I said earlier in the chapter started long before he was allowed to go to school. It was first put in place to devalue him. Than it was to take advantage of him when he was given the opportunity to purchase his freedom during the time of physical slavery. Since he did not know his worth and was unlearned, he had to endure years of labor even after he was freed in order to obtain his freedom from the master behind food, shelter and crop seed for planting. Moreover, since he had no idea through no fault of his owns about the value of money and how to count it, he perhaps paid for his freedom several times over through both money and labor, thus causing him to be in debt in both body and mind. Then when the black man was allowed to go to school, he wasn't taught about money, oh no, the white master wasn't going to have that, because he knew that if the black man became knowledgeable about money than he perhaps would educate his family and better control his earnings. Now, that's just a quick snap shot of the mis-education of the Black man. If you like to read more about the mis-education of the black man, you can read **The Mis-Education of the Negro by Carter G. Woodson for more history.** However, like you read in my introduction at the beginning of this book, WE can no longer blame Charlie Caucasian for our position in live and WE can no longer use slavery as an excuse, because as I have heard talk show radio host and motivational speaker Willie Jolley say; **"You may not be responsible for being knocked down, but you are responsible for getting up."** So black man, stop talking about how you were knocked down and inspire a young brother on how you got up. Now, let us move to today's times. For this mis-education continues to affect us even in today's time. For we are programmed to be consumers rather than producers, a very different vision than what Marcus Garvey had for us. Than when we began to earn a little money and gained an idea of its power, Charlie Caucasian went beyond physical money and developed a planned hardship to what I call, "Get it now and pay for it later", in other words, "CREDIT." Once Charlie Caucasian saw that he could get the money that Joe Johnson has yet to make by allowing him to get the product he wanted now and pay for it at a later date, he know that he now had his Materialistic Slave, hooked, lined and in debt. He taught it to his son Charlie Junior. He saw a gold mine in the making. That gold mine being, "Credit." You have to remember that Charlie Caucasian was well educated in the area of money and finance down through the years and he culturally condition his son Charlie Jr. into thinking that all black folks like shiny things like gold, diamonds, jewelry, rims, cars and what have you and will do whatever it takes to obtain those shiny things. Like I stated earlier, becoming a Materialistic Slave. Now, Charlie Jr. has formed in his mind that if he give the Black man a shiny new shovel ($_{\text{CREDIT CARD}}$) he will dig himself in a hole ($_{\text{DEBT}}$) and bring his gold ($_{\text{MONEY}}$) to master. So, Mr. Charlie extended his "Get it now and pay for it later" plan to Joe Johnson. By doing this, Mr. Charlie saw that his plan had worked and the Black man cared nothing for saving and investing a portion of his earnings for the future, but spent that which he or she could not afford to spend and what's worst, he or she spent that which they have yet to earn, thus keeping them with a shovel in their hands, a hole to dig and bringing his panned gold to Mr. Charlie each month. He saw that Joe Jackson wanted so much to obtain the material items that he himself say Joe you must have, but knew that Joe could not necessarily afford to own, that he were ever so glad to give Joe that shiny new shovel. But once again, like many of us today, Joe was to proud to admit it because most of us want to keep up with the Jones' thinking that they have it going on with the fancy car, the big home and enough bling around his neck that it can be seen from the space station on a sunny day, not knowing that Mr. Jones haven't had a good night's sleep since he got that shiny new shovel in his hand, that new Mercedes- Benz, that ten bedroom home and more gold than Fort Knox hanging around his neck and wrist, simply because Mr. Jones is more into obtaining "THINGS" than he is in educating himself on money, finance and credit. He do not want to live below his means for he rather have his neighbors to say he got it going on than to say Mr. Jones has down sized to fit his income. I want to say this to all those Mr. Jones' out there and to those who may be reading this book. Well, it's not my saying, but GOD's; God says in Proverbs 13:7 **"There's a man that pretends to be rich, yet he is really poor: There's a man that pretends to be poor, yet he is really rich."** Here's the lesson; A poor man cannot live a rich man's life, but on the flip, a rich man can live a poor man's life. The first part of Proverbs 13:7 represents many of us and to be honest, it represented me for many years, but now, I want the second part to represent you and I. However, there are some Mr. Jones' out there that will continue to live out the first part of Proverbs 13:7 and will turn up there nose to Mr. Jackson down the street who has educated himself on money, finance and credit and live within the bounds of his means and sleep in peace every night since he came to the understanding of money and how it works. Mr. Charlie mis-education of Joe Johnson has brainwashed him in his thinking that continues its devastated effect even today and his plan was so effective that even some of his own kind has been swallowed up in this mis-education. However, because of his haughty appetite to feed his greed and power, it had no effect on his conscience. Through his plan of mis-education through the school system in this country, he has created five classes of people according to Keith Cameron Smith, the author of the book (The Top 10 Distinctions between the millionaires and the middle-class) and they are: the very poor; the poor; the middle-class; the rich and the super rich. In addition to that, Mr. Charlie has created a thinking among these classes of people according to the author. The very poor thinks from day to day; The poor thinks from week to week; The middle class thinks from month to month; The rich thinks from year to year and the super rich thinks from decade to decade. Moreover, by allowing him to purchase some of the materialistic products on credit, he now has a consumer for years to come. And his plan to mis-educate the Black man concerning money and finance that he implemented so brilliantly since the day of slavery, he now have a goose with a golden shovel in hand and a community of people who spends an average of $850 to $900 billion per year in this country, some $200 billion more than any other nationality of people according to some economic reports. Just so that you will know, $850 to $900 billion spent by Black America is more than what most third world countries spend as a whole and if we began to educate ourselves, target our money and invest in our own people and businesses, than how much power will we have in this country. But once again, we want "THINGS" like Mr. Jones and not education like Mr. Jackson being in debt to Mr. Charlie. Now look at our kids, for they have no sense of responsibility when it comes to money and finance, because we as parents have no sense of it. When my kids was growing up and was big enough to do chores, they earned my money. I would have them to wash the car and do the lawn with my help of course. When my girls wanted something new, I would explain to them that by earning their own money, they would appreciate the item more because they will take care of it better than they would if I just went out and purchased it for them. Once a child buys something that he or she has worked all day to buy, they will have a very different outlook on loaning it out to friends and family. This builds character and I believe it is a good way for kids at an early age to learn that there are things that's more important than that game boy. This can be your chance to educate your child on saving money and perhaps starting a savings account by taking a percentage of their earnings to invest in their future and learning how to not spend every dime that they make by not becoming a Materialistic Slave. However, we can only pass on that which we know, so my brother, learn about money and finance. Buy books, take some courses and educate yourself for you and your family. There's nothing wrong with having a child earn your money and more parents should visit such an idea, but we give our kids every new trend that comes out soon as they open their mouths, not letting them earn the money by raking people lawns, washing cars and saving their allowance to purchase that new game or bike. Than we wander why our kids value nothing that we buy them. Most black folks say things like. I want my child to have the things my parents couldn't afford me and here's the Black man's golden reason, I don't want my son or daughter to struggle like I had to struggle. If we take the time and look back at history, black folks did more with less money than we are in today's society where we earn more, but are doing less. As I stated earlier, the Black community spends on average $850 billion per year. Now, some would say, man, we're clockin' dollars like that, now that's paper, but to their ignorance, we save less than 5% of our earning and invest less than that. It is time that the Black man start to view money as an important component to the growth of his family. Here's a nugget for you that you may want to give some thought to. You can't afford to buy an item if you cut someone short that you may owe, or take money away from some other bill or obligation that you know that you must pay, like the rent, the car note, the electric bill or any other necessity that you are obligated to each month, than you can't afford that item. But wait, where's my mind, you now have that shovel in your hand, oh, I mean that credit card in your purse or wallet and you pull it out with a smile and give it to the cashier and you walk out the store happy like Gilmore. Now, here's the thing, Mr. Charlie designed the credit card so that you will pay more for the item than you would have if you could have afford to pay cash. In other words, credit makes things cost more and it is design to keep you in debt. But I will say this, credit can be a good thing if we learn how credit works and educate ourselves so that if you do use your credit card to purchase an item, only purchase that which you can afford to pay off in less than thirty days without carrying a balance over. Also, use only half the amount of your credit limit that you have on your card. Here's an example: You have a credit card with a credit limit of $1000, instead of using the whole $1000, use only half or less than half of it, that way on your credit report it will show that you have credit availability and that means the more credit available to you on your card the better your score will be and will build your net wealth and not only that, it will show Mr. Charlie that you are smart. However, if you choose to stay ignorant, than your credit card will become the shovel in your hand and you are digging yourself a hole and giving your gold to master. We in the Black community can no longer be ignorant when it comes down to money and finance and our churches need to step up and have people to come in and educate their congregation on this matter. Black churches takes in billions of dollars each year, but do almost nothing in helping us to become debt free. The pulpit gangsters as I like to call some of them tell us each week about giving our money to help further the kingdom of God, but refuse to instruct or teach us how to become debt free and live a debt free life. That's the freedom we in the black community should strive for, living a debt free life and I do believe that once you and I become that debt free example that others may want to follow and use the principles of the Holy Bible if you believe in the bible as I do, or you may believe in the Holy Koran or whatever holy book you may believe in to stay out of debt, than I believe it will be the greatest sense of freedom that you may experience that is not spiritual.

There are over 2200 references in the bible concerning money, so it must be very important to God, but the only time we hear preachers talk about money is when they send the offer plate around. Now, this is my opinion and if some of you get upset with it, so be it, but as I stated before, I will not find excuses for what I say, but hopefully will give you a reason to why I'm saying it. There are some preachers and pastors out there that do not want their church members to learn about money, finance and/or credit because they want to exploit the uneducated the same way Mr. Charlie has done and is doing. I look at it this way, God knew I was in debt before I surrendered my life to Jesus. He knew that at one point that I too was not educated on money and finance, but through His holy word and reading books and participating in programs, I have become more knowledgeable in the area of money, finance and credit. Now, I may lose some of you here and once again, this is how I see it. Once I have come to the understanding of God's principles when it comes to money and I take those principles, apply them to my life, and get myself out of debt even as I give my offering, than I can give my tithes without strain and give perhaps a greater offering because I'm no longer in debt. I believe that tithing is the fundamental foundation that GOD uses to get us in the spirit of giving without reservation and many of our black churches make their congregation feel guilty if they don't tithe by telling them that if you don't pay your tithes, than you don't trust God to pay your bills. Let me give you an example of this. The electric company tells you that they must have your money on Monday morning at 8:30 or they will cut off your electric at 9:00 am and the only money you have to your name is your tithe offering for the church the Sunday before. Your pastor is up there preaching on tithing and he or she says, God will supply all your needs according to the riches of Christ Jesus. Then he or she say, if you do not give your tithe, God will curse you and not bless you because you do not trust Him to provide for you. Now, the electric company told you that if they do not receive your payment by 8:30 am Monday morning, you will be in the dark at 9:00 am, but the preacher is shouting in your ear this not having faith and not trusting God over and over again that it makes you feel some what guilty for even thinking about using the money to pay your electric bill. So you put your faith and trust in God that He will provide the necessary funds to pay your electric bill and you drop your tithe and your offering in the basket. 9:00 am Monday morning comes around and you are sitting in the dark at your kitchen table counting candles. You go to Mr. Preacher man or Ms. Preacher woman, you explain to them about what happen, and they will tell you that you did not have enough faith and that is the reason why God did not bless you. I'm not telling anyone not to pay their tithes, but some of these pulpit gangsters need to stop making folks feel guilty if they are unable to pay their tithes and I know that some of you bible scholars will say, you shouldn't have an excuse for not paying your tithes, because the bible say that God get the first ten percent of your earnings and some would even say that if you do not tithe, you will go to hell. Well, my comeback to that statement is this, God knew I was in debt before He saved me and he knows that I'm in debt while I'm now saved and He knows that I have to implement His principles in my life to get out of debt and be debt free. Another thing that I want to make clear right here, right now is that tithing is not a give to get scheme as many pulpit gangsters make it out to be, but as I have stated before, tithing in my opinion is the fundamental foundation that GOD uses to get us in the spirit of giving freely without reservation, not some crafty way of thinking that we can trick GOD into I gave to the church, so YOU give more back to me. Many of us in the black community need to throw off that coat of pride that no one can tell us how to spend our money, even the money we yet to make, because there are some folks out there that can help you to manage your finances a lot better than what you are doing. However, to be honest, many of us is in the shape that we are in simply because of PRIDE. Followed by our lack of knowledge and understanding when it comes to money and finance. If some of us were to be bless with the winning numbers to the lotto, most of us would be paralyze broke within a two-year period simply because we are ignorant when it comes down to money. We would spend ourselves broke. Here is another nugget for you to think about, if you cannot control the $100 in your wallet or purse now, than how can you control $100,000. Instead of you controlling the money, the money will be controlling you. I have had family members and friends who had come into some money and like so many of us who is Boo-boo the Fool, they couldn't begin to tell you where the money gotten to. I would tell them that they must have sold their money. That's a phrase that I use quite often, especially when you have those folks who get paid on Friday morning at 9:00 am and paralyzed broke by 9:30 am and do not have a clue to where their check went. We need to learn all that we can about money and we need to pass that education on to our kids and teach our kids how to build wealth and what assets it takes to build wealth. Just so some of you may know, your car is not an asset; for it depreciates in value once you drive it off the car lot. Another thing that you should know that the bankers and the loan officers will not tell you is that your house is not an asset and I know that some of you may be saying that clearly this guy do not know what the hell he's talking about. Well, let me educate you. An asset is something that generates a positive stream of income. It puts money in your pocket. That Cadillac that is sitting in your driveway is not an asset and I tell you why it is not. You pay a monthly payment each month on it, therefore it cost you money each month to own it. So, that Cadillac is not an asset, but, a liability. I will explain liability to you. A liability is something that takes money out of your pocket and do not produce a positive stream of income. Now I know that the banker or loan officer told you that your home is your biggest asset and to a degree, they are right. However, they fail to tell you that it's an asset to them and the bank because you pay a mortgage each month to them and it is generating a positive stream of income for the bank and it is a liability for you because it costing you money each month and the only time it will become an asset for you is when it is paid for and it appreciates in value over time and you sell it for a profit or rent it out and your rental fee is more than your monthly expenses, than it becomes an asset. So remember, an asset produce money, a liability takes away money. And now you know. Have you ever given it any thought, that there are far less Jews in this country than there are African Americans, but according to some reports, they control more than 40 percent of the money in this country. The Jews teach their kids about money perhaps more than the White man perhaps and he teaches his child not to be so materialistic. The Black man teaches his child almost nothing in this area as a whole. It's funny that according to some statistics, a person coming over from a foreign country is four times more likely to become a millionaire than a Black man who is born in this country. Wow, that is something to think about. Let's take a look at the difference between the mind set we pass on to our kids and the mind set the Jew man and the White man pass on to their kid(s) because money literacy is a must in their household. I use this example a lot when I talk to young kids and some adults. First, we have the black youth, age 15, just starting high school. He was given

$1500.00 to purchase clothes for the school year. He goes to the mall for a day of shopping and on the first day of school, he is dressed in the latest gear from head to toe. I'm talking Air Jordan's sneakers, Coogie jeans, Roca Wear shirt, baseball cap, gold watch, necklace and arm bracelet. His name brand attire left him blank in his pocket, but hey, he's looking good is what most black folks would say. The Jew kid is given the same amount of money for the very same reason, but instead of buying the name brand items, he just buys normal clothes that cost around $900.00 dollars total. The Black kid walks up to his Jew friend and laugh at his clothes because they are not name brand. He than tell his friend that he spent $1500.00 plus dollars on his clothes, not giving thought that he is paralyze broke in his pocket, but hey, he looks good. The Jew kid says he spent $900.00 on his clothes because he did not need to wear the names brand clothes. He made a deposit of $550.00 in the bank and kept the balance in his pocket. The Black kid tell the Jew kid how good he look in his clothes, but is ignorant to the fact that he is paralyze broke and the Jew kid tells him that I may not have the name brand clothes as you, but I have a bank account in my name and while you spend all your money on things that has no value, my money is earning interest and I'm not broke. As you can see, we pass our ignorance on to our kids and they do not prepare for tomorrow, but spend everything they earn today. We have to do better Black man. But hey, who the hell am I to say something about his people? Than some may wander to why I ask the question, So, what's wrong Black man? And the answer is =ME.

Ch. 6 - Family:
A designed separation

Another reason to why we are in the shape that we are in is that we have lost the importance of family in my opinion. Once again, I believe that this is done by design and we are too blind to see that the black family is being attacked from all directions. This is nothing new, for the black man and his family has always been attacked since the days of slavery. Because of greed, power and an indwelling evil that took up residence in the heart of many White Europeans that came over on ships, journeyed to the black continent of Africa and found that the black man was the perfect commodity to own at a cheap price to build his new world, simply because he has develop the mindset that he is superior in every area of humanity and perhaps elevated himself to the reign of GOD. But we also must remember that history tells us that all the blame cannot be placed on the white man alone, because tribal leaders also played a significant part in the slave trade and the separation of the unified black family. For many black men were sold into slavery by the very people who was of the same complexion as him. He was separated from his family without remorse, taken from his home land in chains and shackles by brutal force and that bond to his family's soil was broken and only remembered by the tears that he shade in the belly of the slave ships as the land that sustained his family for generations has become faded in the distance as the slave ships sailed to a land that he never imagine he would ever be. The black man's family was his bond to the universe. It was the one source that gave the black man his identity and gave him his self worth and an image that he was no mistake as to why he were placed on this side of heaven. You may not believe in the West Indies slave master Willie Lynch and his letters detailing to the white slave masters in this country how to control their slaves for years to come by putting them against one another, programming them through an abuse method that they would only trust the white man and separate him from his family. However, whether it is true or false, you cannot deny that we are doing the very same thing today that is written in the letters of Willie Lynch, which I encourage all black men to read. He gives precise details on how he has studied the Negro man and the Negro woman and the bond that they hold for one another and family. He knew that in order for the black man to summit his will to his will, he must first break the bond that the black man has for his family. He gave speeches that if the white slave masters were to separate the two, put the young Negro slave against the old Negro slave, the dark skinned slave against the light skinned slave and strip the adult Negro slave of his family responsibilities by beating him in front of his wife and child, then it will be the Negro woman who will take over his responsibilities. He talked about that if his methods are followed, the success of his methods will go on for some three hundred plus years. This is just a quick summary of what has been done to the black man down through the years and you can read the letters for yourself by visiting (www.willielynchletters.com) and if you look at it, we are fulfilling his method on a daily basis even in this day and time. The way I see it is that black folks has not been together since the civil rights movement and we are more apart today than we were yesterday and sometimes it seems that tomorrow will have an even bigger gap. We have gotten to the point that we have become prejudice against ourselves within our own community by finding some kind of flaw with one another based on skin tone, hair, weight, height, eat meat, don't eat meat and so on. This is for all you perfect folks who may have this internal prejudice dwelling inside of you. Unless you are Jesus Christ himself, you are perfectly flawed. Some family members have stopped speaking to one another over some of the most ridicules reasons like education, social status and success. When was the last time you seen a black family sit down at the dinner table and ate together? Family time eating together was sacred back in the day among the black family. It was a time when family members would come together, talk about there day and prepare for tomorrow. A time when kids would tell their parents what they learned in school, discuss their dreams, hopes and aspirations. A time when a parent would ask their child what they hope to be when they grow up. A time when a father would fulfill that old Chinese proverb that goes like this **(Give a man a fish and you will feed him for a day, teach him how to fish and you will feed him for a life time)** That was a time when fathers would teach their sons how to be a men, respect their mother and women, how to raise a family, take pride in their community and meet their responsibility to the family. A time when mothers would teach their daughters how to conduct themselves as women, run a household, cook, clean and have high moral value. To a degree, we do not have those types of parents anymore, simply because as I have stated earlier, look at the parents of today, they are children having children. Now you can see to why family togetherness around the dinner table has gone out the door just like the front porch talks of old, where children would sit for hours at a time listening to their parents and grandparents tell stories of bravery, faith, unity and love. There were more stories told on the front porch of black folks homes than there were stories written in a book. We have gotten so that it's no longer important to have that family conversation anymore and to keep it very real, it seems that the only time black folks do come together is at a funeral or some type of beer party, and that is a damn shame. But hey, who am I to say something about his people? Here's another thing that the black man and woman do more than most, they complain about everything but many will not move a finger to bring about change. We have yet to realize that it only takes one act of random kindness (ARK) to bring forth a positive change in our community. But to be honest, I'm not sure if I can say that we have a community the way that the black family conducts itself now a days. Rather, it may be safe to say that we have just a neighborhood, for a community has unity, compassion and a willingness to do, even when others turn away. This statement reminds me of the little story that I must have read a hundred times called, **Everybody, Somebody, Anybody and Nobody** and it goes a little something like this: **(This is a little story of four people named, Everybody, Somebody, Anybody and Nobody. There was an important job to be done and Everybody was sure that Somebody would do it. Anybody could have done it, but Nobody did it. Somebody got angry about that because it was Everybody's**

job. Everybody thought that Anybody could do it, but Nobody realized that Everybody wouldn't do it. It ended up that Everybody blamed Somebody when Nobody did what Anybody could have done.) There is a lot of truth in this comedy story. The black family has become so separated that we sit around and wait for the next man to do something that would benefit us as a whole rather than to get up off our rusty dusty and do it ourselves. Than when someone does decide to do something, than some of us have the audacity to speak ill of that person. Will the black man and his family ever come together? As long as we continue our complaining and never to come together as a people; unified in love, strong in numbers and brave in heart, than we will always be looked at by other races as a load joke and a do nothing people. Let me lay this on you, other folks that are not your color is used to your rambling off at the mouth. Hell, the Godfather of soul, James Brown in my opinion perhaps got sick and tired of our complaining so much that he himself made a song about it called **"Talking loud and saying nothing."** Many of us are the very fulfillment of the songs title, talking loud and saying absolutely nothing. They have come to understand that all we're going to do is complain, complain and complain. And never doing a damn thing about that which we complain about because they have come to realize that the plan to keep us apart years ago are still active even today and we are fulfilling that which they were taught and what we were culturally condition to perform. The white man looks at the black family as a treat, for he knows that if the black man and his family ever come together throughout this land, he is a force. How can he not be, look at all he has endued in this country from slavery, denied education, the civil rights movement, unjust laws, Jim Crow, drugs placed in the black community, the Tuskegee Experiment, the assassination of Black leaders and he's still here. Not only is he still here, but he is President of this above GOD nation. However, he has forgotten what brought him this far. God first, family second and coming together as a people third. Now many of us would say that we as a black community has come a long ways since the days of slavery and I would agree. However, we must look at the picture in its entirety and have the understanding that Charlie Caucasian has come a long ways, perhaps even more so than Joe Johnson. Joe Johnson can get things done because of the stock that he comes from and he has the patience to hang in there until his change come, but than again, the black man and the black family of today is not the same black man and black family of yesterday, for today we stand for nothing but will lay down for anything. And once again I will say this, I do believe that the separation of the black family is design to keep us fighting against one another and we as black people need to stop all the internal prejudice and dislike we have towards one another. Internal prejudice is the statement I choose to use because it seems that we have this self hatred towards one another much like that of the Mulattoes doing the Haiti revolt and we have gotten to the point that it no longer bother our conscience nor disturb our soul when we see young folks emulating that in which they see among their elders. Look at the condition of our homes today. We no longer see that togetherness that was exemplified back in the day. Many of our homes today are no longer homes to many of our young people, but empty shelters. Parents are hooked on drugs and do not give a damn how their abuse affect their child. Many turn to drugs to fill the emptiness that escape is just a hit away. Escape from the reality of their choices in life. Escape from having children's. Escape from the pain of a broken family. Escape from the truth about themselves so that they can continue to live the lie that makes them feel somewhat good about themselves. There are so many kids in the black community that dread going home, seeing their mom wasted on the couch from smoking crack cocaine and dad paralyze drunk from drinking all day if they are so lucky that they even have a dad in the home. But hey, who am I to say something about his people? Many of our young people who want to make something of themselves are coming home to homes that are nasty and filthy. Many do not have a decent place in the home to study and/or do home work, than when some of these parents see that their child are trying to do something with their life, they say things like; why are you studying that for, you going to mount up to nothing just like me, or, they will say things that will discourage the child because they chose to do nothing with their life. Some will go as far as to tell their sons that they are no count just like their father instead of telling them that they are better than their father because they have a problem with the dad or the mom if you are a man saying this to your daughter. A child should come home to a house of love, peace and tranquility, not a house of hell as many do. If no one has even told you, we are a better people than that and we really do need to get it together. Back in the day, folks looked out for one another. When you had a problem, I had a problem was the Neighbor's Creed, but now it's more like, your problem is just that, your problem. Where have our compassion gone? that old saying, it takes a village to raise a child is no longer in our vocabulary, because that village of unity is now a faded memory of our past and we have no desire to recapture that unity again because we have become selfish in our ways and in our thinking. But once again, who am I to say something about his people? Than some may wander to why I ask the question, So, What's wrong Black Man? And the answer is = ME

Ch. 7 - Justice System:
A perfect profit to jail you

Many of us do not know that the justice system in this country is tied into the educational system. Some may say how is this statement true and what makes the justice system and the educational system in someway partners? Well, I'm glad you ask. The justice system determine how many jails and prisons to build based on your child's third grade reading ability and from that they calculate to whether to build new housing quarters for your sons and daughters. There are tests given over your child's early schooling by those who study human behavior in children that they can determine if Little John John or Little Ms. Precious will turn out to be an outstanding citizen or a moneymaking prison or jail slave. There is a prison industrial complex in this country and it stems from the educational system because there is so much money to be made when you are locked up. Did you know that at one point, there were a very small percentage of privately funded jails and prisons in this country and now there are over some several dozen privately operated prisons that generate hundred of millions of dollars per year, if not billions? The privatization of prisons are so big of a business in this corporate capitalized country of ours that I wouldn't be surprise that they are not on the New York Stock Exchange. In fact, it has become so profitable that you now have Judges, Lawyers, Engineers, Doctors, CEO,s and even down to your everyday private citizen that are investing big money in this growing greed to house you and your child. Look at corporations like Wackenhut. They are perhaps the largest entity along with Corrections Corporation of America (CCA) in the private prison industry, operating more than half of the industry's operation. If you want to see your worth in being locked up, here are some old figures you can nibble on. In 1992, Wackenhut earned more than 630 million dollars and I'm sure that amount has drastically grown over the years. Corrections Corporation of America was founded in 1983 by investors behind Kentucky Fried Chicken (KFC), the connections of former Republican Party chair Tom Beasley and the sell skills of Nashville banker/ financier Dr. Crants to win contracts to operate the INS detention centers. Once again black man; there is BIG money in locking you up. Just to give you some idea just how the United States rates among other countries as far as locking up there citizens. At the beginning of President Ronald Reagan's presidency, there were fewer than 400,000 inmates incarcerated in the U.S. prisons and jails. Today there are more than 2.2 million. Out of that number, more than 1.2 million are black men. Followed by Hispanics and others. The U.S. house more people per capital than any other country on the planet, yet, crime over all has not decreased and billions of dollars are being spent to keep you as a 21st. century slave. Yes, you heard me right, I said 21st. century slave. When you are incarcerated, by law you are officially a slave. The 13th. Amendment states this: **Neither slavery nor involuntary servitude, EXCEPT as a punishment for crime where of the party shall have been duly convicted, shall exist within the United States nor any place subject to their jurisdiction.** That means that according to the 13th. Amendment of the U.S. constitution, any person that are imprisoned for a crime, the state and the government has the law behind them to make you a slave and have you work for pennies a day on jobs that if you were not incarcerated, would probably pay you several dollars per hour. There are two kinds of justice systems in America, one for Mr. Charlie and the other for Joe Johnson. You would have to be totally blind or from another planet if you think for one second that there are not. I know that some of you may be thinking that this is a false statement and unconstitutional, but you have to remember that the constitution was written by and for Mr. Charlie, not Joe Johnson. And this country has gotten so far from the constitution, that all those bought and paid for Politian's do not have a clue to what the constitution say or do not say. Here's another fact shocker for you. Black girls are being locked up at a faster rate than black men these days and black men are subject to a higher penalty than a white man who commits the same offense. How is it that Blacks and Hispanics in this country makes up only 25% of the population, but, make up more than 50% of the prison population? I'll tell you how, there's big profit in locking you up and we in the black community are making it easy for them to do so by the selling of drugs, the raping of our black queens, the gang activities, the robbing and stealing of things that does not belong to us and the senseless murders of our people and other nationalities. We can no longer continue this way of living and expect equal justice in a white man's system. If you give it some thought, the justice system is designed to incarcerate as many blacks as it can. This country and its above GOD government has come up with another way to keep slavery alive and well by the way of the penal system. I want to take the time to drop this on you my black man friend. Why is it that when a black man get caught with the same amount of crack cocaine that a white man have in powdered cocaine, he is sentence more harse than the white man? I'll tell you just incase you do not know. Crack cocaine is consider a black man's drug, yet it takes powdered cocaine to make it, however, because society looks at it as a black man's drug he or she is sentence to a more stiffer penalty then there white counterpart and we know that many laws in this country is designed to house as many blacks as possible. Those in power made the ratio of crack cocaine a 100:1 ratio, thus making those caught with crack cocaine to pay a much higher penalty. Now, if you were to flip it the other way and crack cocaine was a White man's drug and powdered cocaine was that of the Black man, than powdered cocaine would net Joe Johnson a much stiffer penalty than what Mr. Charlie would receive from his crack cocaine in the same amount simply because, no matter which drug, whether it is crack or powdered cocaine, once it is labeled as the black man's drug, he will receive the heaviest penalty, simply because he is a Black man. When will we wake up from this nightmare and realize that we are better than what is said about us on television and what is written about us in the papers and magazines. When you go to prison, as I said earlier, by law you will be looked at as a slave and worked like one also. You will work an average of 8 hours per day and be paid slave wages that range from 0.20 cents to perhaps $2.50 per hour, 40 hours per week on jobs that earned the prison thousands of dollars. There are corporations like General Electric and Delco Remy that uses the prisons in the federal system to make parts for motors and other equipment under the name UNICOR. It maybe safe to say that these jobs that prisoners are doing for pennies probably pay in the neighborhood of $12 to $17 dollars per hour if performed outside the prison system. These are just two major companies that use the prison system of the federal government to earn huge profits from slave wages and labor. Now, for some of you who are so naive' into thinking that we are beyond all this unequal justice and racism in this so-called Christian country of ours just because we have a black president, you are sadly mistaken. There are just as much injustice going on now than before. Black men and young black boys are being shot in their backs in unjustified shootings by white officers, some shoot more than 30, 40, and 50 times and the SHOOT NOW and because I'm WHITE, I don't have to answer questions later police officers are not being persecuted by the courts and the ALL WHITE juries are justifying these shootings as if those who are being shot and killed are sport. But yet, a lot of us want to believe what Mr. Charlie say, when he say that this country was founded on Christian morals and the bible. You may believe that B.S. if you choose to, but my take on this is that this country is no more a Christian nation than the devil himself is and what bible is Charlie Caucasian basing his saying on, surely it's not the bible that I read and study. Another thing that you should think about when it comes to the un-justice system in this country is that when you are a black man going to court for a crime, you ARE guilty until proven innocent. Yeah Yeah, I know what you may be saying, he written that down wrong, it should read, you are innocent until proven guilty, no, you read it correctly and I will explain it this way. Television, radio, newspapers, magazines and racism had made the black man to not only look guilty in the eyes of our court system, but to be guilty. The saying that you have become so accustom to hearing, You are innocent until proven guilty is not the saying for the black man in my opinion, but that for the white man. Now, I will admit to you that you will probably not hear some D.A. or some federal U.S. attorney tell you what you just read, but I will assure you, it's true and black man, I hope that you will remember that the laws in this country was not written for you, but written against you. You who are reading this book may say to yourself, how do this guy know about what is the pay in some of these prisons and what companies use the prison system to manufacture some of its products? I'm glad you ask. The author of this book have had personal experience. You see, I made a decision back in 2002 that landed me in federal lock-up at a Low facility and a camp for $3^{1/2}$ years and I worked on a job for the Department of Agricultural. My job along with others was to maintain and preserve the historic sites of the civil war. Build hiking trails and help to maintain visitor centers for tourist. I was told by my supervisor that the job that we were doing paid $17.00 per hour if we were out in the streets, but since we were in federal lock-up, we were paid 17 cents to start and at the end of 30 days, we got a big pay raise to the sum of a whooping 28 cents per hour. Now, I know you want to stop reading right here and run and get your calculator to find out just what these figures may come out to be. Let me spare you the pain. I worked 8 hours per day for 17 cents with weather permitting. Here's the breakdown; 17 x 8= $1.36 per day; $6.80 per week; $20.40 per month;   Now, for the big raise. 28 x 8= $2.24 per day; $11.20 per week; $44.80 per month on a job that paid $17.00 per hour out in society. But here's the kicker, some of these young black guys would often tell me that they wouldn't work for McDonalds', Burger King, Popeye's Chicken or some other type of job that perhaps pays $5.00 per hour and I tell them that if you do not stop selling those drugs, stop stealing, stop breaking in folks homes and stop all the gang activities, the very thing that you claim you won't do will be the very thing you will be doing and it will give you a whole new outlook on that $5.00 per hour gig that McDonalds' once offered. So, as you can see, there is a perfect profit to house you and your kids, so if I were you, I will talk to my son and/or daughter, brother or sister, my niece or nephew, my aunt or uncle, my cousin and friend to let them know that the system care nothing about them other than wanting their labor to make them a perfect profit. We in the black community have to get a hold on this going to jail and prison thing and we adults have to talk to our young people about making bad decisions that will cause them to enter prison or jail. If you think about it, the black man in this country has a big red target on his back and there are some Mr. Charlie's out there who will try everything in his power to stop his progress, to keep him from moving forward and one of those ways is to jail you and me for long periods of time and by doing so, the jailing of you and I not only separate us from our family and love ones, but will stop our growth in producing children's and expanding our community. We need to see the truth in this day and time behind the prison industrial complex in this country, that it's not all about housing the criminals as it was back in the day, but turning a perfect profit. The in-justice system in this so-called Christian nation of ours continue to preach that same old lie that prison is to rehabilitate the prisoner into a better person, but yet most prisons in this country treat there incarcerated like common dogs. A large part of the problem with the in-justice system in this country is the courts. As I have stated earlier, there are some judges that are sitting on the bench, handing out unjustified sentences to black men both young and old that are receiving kickbacks in the thousands from some of these prisons. That B.S. lie that Lady Justice in this country is balance and blind when it comes down to the law and the citizens of this nation truly is a bunch of bull, she may have a blindfold over one of her eyes to give the impression that she sees no color, have no bias and is fair and balance, but that's all a lie, because once again I will say this, in this so-called Christian nation of ours, a Black man is guilty in the eyes of Mr. Charlie's courthouse until proven innocent and if you choose not to believe it, just visit your local courthouse on your next day off. Another thing that is troublesome about this un-justice system we have is that the punishment doesn't always fit the crime or offense. I'll speak on the federal side since I do know a little something about it. There are some good and decent judges out there that if they had the discretionary power that they once had, they would apply the punishment to fit the crime or offense. They could take in consideration the accursed person situation to why they committed such an offense. They could take in consideration if that person can be rehabilitated and the cost it will cost the government to have that person incarcerated. They could take in consideration if justice is best served by a long sentence to be carried out or by some other type of intervention that could be used as an alternative. But since our brought and paid for congress scripted them of this power and replaced it with mandatory minimum guidelines that was to be only for the mafia cartel, now every person that is bought before the federal bench is subject to these guidelines and it's unfair that a young person who has never been in any kind of trouble before, who has committed a non-violence offense can been sentence to a long sentence the same as someone who has taken a life, but we continue to believe that the laws in this so-called Christian nation are fair. Black man, we have to stop putting ourselves in situations that will cause us to make decisions that will put us in front of some of these kickback judges and

D.A.'s that are earning thousands of dollars by sending you to jail for long periods of time just so you can make them millions of dollars. Let me give you a little insight on the money it takes to house you and maybe by it you will have a better idea on what I'm saying to you so that you won't become a 13th. Amendment slave. When I was incarcerated, the government paid the local jail that housed me $130.00 per day for 116 days that totaled $15,080. It took only $2.25 per day to feed me. I had to buy my own under clothes, socks, shoes and health products, so as you can see, the jail profited $127.25 per day for a federal inmate and I was told that the jail was paid $105.00 per day to house state inmates and the profit was $102.75 per day. Now, if you think that there is not a perfect profit to jail you, then look at this. When I was incarcerated, I read that it took $37,000 to $40,000 per year to keep a federal inmate locked up and if you had some kind of health problem, it took upward of $60,000 per year, which I believe is a bunch of B.S. because the prison system is not designed to lose money, but to turn a profit, so for the sake of argument I will entertain this myth or atleast look at it in the light that these figures may represent the cost of officers, vehicles, equipment, electricity, heating gas and other expenses. Now, if the federal government is willing to pay this dollar amount per year to house me, just how much do you think I made them and their cronies from my slave labor? Well, once again, I will save you the time so that you do not have to put the book down to get your calculator. So lets go back to what I said earlier. I will use the highest paid wage for this, so here we go; I was paid 28 cents per hour for 8 hours per day, 5 days per week, 20 days per month, 12 months a year for the total dollar amount of $537.60 per year. Now, I was told by my work supervisor that that job paid $17.00 per hour, so here's my example: 8 hours x $17.00= $136.00 per day; 5x $136.00= $680.00 per week; 4 weeks per month=$2720.00; 12 months x $2720.00= $32,640 per year, yet I was paid $537.60 per year and here's the perfect profit, $32,102.40 net. The government got a $32,600 a year job done for $537.00 a year, saving the Department of Agricultural thousands of dollars per year and there was 8 of us, not only did we save them money as for as salary goes because they did not have to hirer 8 civilians, but also saved them money on health care if they were to hire everyday people to do the jobs we were doing. Please, do not be so gullible that you believe everything that this crooked government report to you. Do you not know that this government of ours are the biggest crooks in this country in my opinion and for me personally, I do not trust any of them in Washington D.C., from the President all the way down to the dogcatcher. In my opinion, all of them are opportunists and liars, because every time they take a breath they breathe out lies. They lie about what's really going on with this so- called Christian nation of ours. They are crooks, because they cut under handed deals with those who mean us no good, not doing the will of the people who voted them into office, but doing their own selfish will that they know the people may be against. They are money worshippers because they chase the dollar and walk hand-in-hand with lobbyist who they say that they will never be partners with and care for nothing but their own well-being. Please don't think that those folks in D.C. are any better than you, for they are not, most of them have a record of drunk-driving, spousal abuse, traffic violations, criminal activity and suspended driver license. As I have said, the biggest crooks in this country in my opinion are located in D.C., not behind prison walls. Do not be afraid of those behind prison walls because they can't hurt you. The ones who we should be afraid of are those in D.C. and on Wall Street, for they truly are the GANGSTERS. And let me say this, if you think that the government is running this country, than you are brainwashed. For the government haven't ran this country for years because the BIG CORPORATIONS makes all the decisions and laws in this country. Corporations knows that D.C. has a need for GREED and they feed that greed with hundred of millions of dollars per year to get things done that will benefit them and not the people. If this was not true, than why won't congress pass a law to band lobbyists? I'll tell you why they wouldn't dare try to band lobbyists, because that's where their butter comes from to butter their toast. Most Politian's that goes to D.C. in the beginning started out with good intentions, they had the wiliness to help the people that elected them to office, they had a heart for the people, to better the lives of their constituents, but once they got there, tasted the sweet of the water and ate the fat of the land, their heart of flesh turned to a heart of stone and once they saw that they could have another GOD that had the power to make things happen for them personally, one they could believe in and I'm not talking about the one that most of us believe who sits on a throne in heaven, they forgot about the promises they made on the campaign trail and the hope that they gave to the voters. In other words, their new GOD have revealed himself in several faces and you know them also, Washington, Lincoln, Hamilton, Jackson, Grant and Franklin. But, who am I to say something about our brought and paid for elected officials? The famous poet Maya Angelo had a saying those goes; "When you know better, you do better." All she is saying is that once you gain the understanding of something, brake it down to its core and know how to apply the good of it to your life to better empower you, than you have obtained the power to do better all around. Now, once you have gain this understanding, you can't hoard it for only yourself, but you have the obligation to share it with other folks that they too may gain a better understanding to do better. Black man, we are going to jail and prison at two to three times the rate as white's and it same as if we see nothing wrong with that. I will say it again and again, there is a perfect profit to jail you and when you do something stupid out in the community and end up in jail or prison, there's a good chance that that judge to whom you are now standing in front of, just might have a monetary reason to give you some jail time and a new 911 address. Remember what I said earlier, there are many professional people who are investing thousands of dollars in private prisons and if we continue on the path that many of us is traveling, than why shouldn't they, when they see that they can continue to mass incarcerate black people no matter have unjustified it may be. Mr. Charlie has implemented a new way to keep slavery alive and well and we are contributing to our own demise. Our young black boys shouldn't be getting their High School diploma or GED from jail or prison, but from school and colleges. Most of these so- called drug runners don't have a clue to what damage they are doing to themselves and their people. They do not know that once you become a felony on the state or federal level, you have that tag for live and you are looked at as a disease among a healthy community. When you have that flag on your forehead, you can be discriminated against for housing, loans, food stamps, employment, healthcare and other things and you have former President Bill Clinton to thank for that. For it was he who signed into law these very things and for all of you who are still drinking the Clinton Kool-aid, do you not know that under his administration, there were more black men locked-up under his Presidency than any other President before him and as I just mention, he made it so that you can be legally discriminated against when you commit an offense even if it's non-violence and you are a first time offender. You must realize that the system is set up in a way that once you do your time for whatever you may have committed, it wants you to return back to the system so that you can continue to earn the share holders that perfect profit and even though those in power regurgitate the same B.S. lie over and over again that once you fulfill your debt to society and are rehabilitated, all is well, Bull****. Your debt is never paid and the un-justice system will let you know just that. The system does not care if you are a first time non-violence young person who may have had a dime bag of drugs on your person when they caught you, all the system sees is that you are legally a 13th. Amendment slave for the next several months or years and when you are released from jail or prison, you are not released from the system even if you are not on papers. Young black boys do not know that there's a prefect profit to jail them and the system goes well beyond the prison walls, so let me drop this information on you in hope that what you are reading will give you a new way of thinking and a spirit to share with your love ones. I'm speaking on the federal level once again. After you have satisfied your sentence in the federal system, to help you adapt back to society, they offer you a 2 – 6 month halfway house depending on the sentence you received. Once you get a job, one of the rules that you must follow is that you will have to give 25 percent of your pay to the halfway house each pay period and this is done before taxes. Here's an example to give you a better understanding: You work 40 hrs. per week at $10.00 per hour, that's $400.00 per week before taxes. You have to give the halfway house $100.00 each week the whole time you are under the halfway house program and it does not matter if you do some of your halfway house time at home, you still have to pay. Once again, there's a perfect profit to jail you and your child. I was locked up with guys who made a ton of money, I mean a ton of money and I would ask them, was the money and this time that you are doing worth being away from your family and friends? And there answer would always be, HELL NO!!! There were guys who had sentences of 5- 30 years and the Fed's don't give a damn if you are young or old, healthy or sick, family or no family, it does not care about any of that, it only care about there time. So you will know, the Fed's do not sentence you in years, they sentence you in months, it's up to you to figure out the months in years. If you are sentence to 360 months, than guess what, you have 30 years. My cell mate was a young guy who was sentence to 212 months, that's 17 years 8 months. When I was released in 2005, he still had 8 years to go. Another friend of mines was at one point sentence to 960 months, that's 80 years. He's out now and doing well and you may be thinking, how is he home with that kind of sentence? I leave that thinking up to you to figure out. However, I will say this to you, on the federal side, the first one who talks gets the deal and for you guys who makes the claim that you are HARD CORE, I'm no punk and will not tell on your boy no matter what, I will say this to you. When your boy hear you say that no matter what goes down, I will not say a word about you and you do the same for me. I will do the time and I will have to admit, sometimes because of the people to whom you may be involved with, you may have to do just that because they may do some harm to your family and love ones. But I'm not talking about those kind of people. The people I'm talking about are the local fish that are swimming in the small pond and when you and your boy get hit up and you both are sitting in separate rooms at DEA central and your boy remember the words that you have always said from day one that no matter what happens, you will keep your mouth shut. So, let me tell you what your boy is doing over in the next room. He's over there preparing for a concert, because he is going to sing like Aretha Franklin at an opera house while you are over there being HARD or like the late Bernie Mac would say, a new FOOL. So remember what I said, on the federal side, the first person that talks get the deal. I was invited to speak at my church not long after my release to talk to the young people about my experience at a federal low and camp and I told those so- called hard wanna be thugs about some of the guys I met and told of their stories of how they would always say that they would never tell on their boy if they ever got caught and I will let you know this and you can take it anyway you like I told them. Almost all of them said that they wish that they have told on their boy first because the very thing that they said that they wouldn't do, their homeboy did and he's out and they' re still serving time. Of course you had some of the little knuckle heads that was in the audience saying that they are no punk or a snitch, and my response to that was what I stated earlier to what the late Bernie Mac once said, "No, You are not a punk, you are a new fool, because I be damn if I'm going to do your time for your crime." Young black boys that is out there slinging that dope better know that that home boy who they are running around with ever get himself caught up, he will not only tell lies on YOU, but some will tell lies on JESUS CHRIST

HIMSELF to get that weight off of them. Once again, the Fed's have a saying, the first to talk gets the deal and that's the gospel. This will be my last true example of what I said about what you just read. Another guy that I knew at the low facility before I was transferred to the camp told on his whole family, I mean he told on his dad, his mom, his sister, a brother and a friend. He had a sentence of more than 25 years dropped down to 9 years and the fed's do not care who you tell on, there are in the business of locking you up, PERIOD. And they are quick to tell you, we care nothing about your family, because you didn't care about them, for if you did, you wouldn't be here with us now, would you? THERE IS A PERFECT PROFIT TO JAIL YOU, BELIEVE THAT. All it takes is for the love of one person to stand up and say, I love my people to much to continue to sit on my tootie fruity and watch the atrocity against my people to progress on. We cannot afford to lose a generation of our young people to the madness that is going on in our community, nor can America afford to lose such a large human commodity itself. This nation and its government have a lot to answer for, but so do WE as a people also. We have to encourage our young blacks to glamorize education, not stupidity. Glamorize smart decisions in life, not life costing ones. Glamorize family unity, not gang activity. Glamorize staying out of prison, not entering in as if it's a badge of honor. Glamorize self-love, not internal hate, Glamorize the uplifting of a people, not the tearing down of one, Glamorize the Power of GOD, not the work of the devil, Glamorize making Black history, not becoming a Black Death mystery. But hey, who the hell am I to say something about his people? I'll tell you who I am. I'm the guy who truly loves his people and that mean ALL PEOPLE. I'm the guy who will no longer sit back with his hand tuck between his legs, a blind fold over his eyes, plugs in his ears just so that he can have a punk ass excuse to do nothing and say nothing to the destruction of his people. I'm the guy who will tell folks on both sides about the goodness that lies in the heart of the BLACK MAN and I'm the guy who will share with his follow man the power of JESUS CHRIST. Than some may wander to why I ask the question, **So, what's wrong Black man?** And the answer is= NOT JUST YOU, BUT ALSO ME.

Ch. 8 - Charlie Caucasian:
The meaning behind of the name

Many of you may be thinking what is the meaning behind the name Charlie Caucasian or how I came up with the name. Well let me tell you. The name Charlie Caucasian was first mention to me by my cousin Bennie Smith down in Atlanta, Ga. and once I heard it I knew it was the perfect name I should use in my book. It is the titled name that we both agreed to when it comes down to those White folks who continue the ways and beliefs of White supremacy. Those who have a deep seeded hatred without cause and a dis-like trust without reason for the Joe Johnson's in this country because his skin tone is different from his. He is that person who no longer hides behind the hooded mask that keeps his identity a secret, but that person who sits on the bench in our nations courtrooms and hand out unjust sentences to those person of color when they perhaps deserves a tap on the hand rather than a paddle on their ass and on the flip, Charlie Jr. receive a stern talking to or probation for the same offense. He's that White man or White woman who will give Charlie Jr. a job who has a criminal record and perhaps only a high-school degree before Joe Johnson who has a college degree and no record. That White banker who charges Joe Johnson a higher rate than that of Charlie Jr. even if they both have the same credit rating, or charge Mr. Johnson more for a car than someone of his own complexion. That lawmaker who sits behind the desk of our local, state and federal offices who introduce laws that is subjective towards one race of people and objective to another because they share the same complexion. Caucasian describes the complexion of the White man as a whole and Charlie was chosen simply because it fits so well with Caucasian, thus coming up with the name Charlie Caucasian. This name in no way describes or label all White folks as a Charlie Caucasian, only those who rightly fit and fulfill the meaning that I describe him or her to be. Charlie Caucasian are those White folks who teach and train their kids to be racist solely based on the color of ones skin, hating folks without reason. He is that person who is afraid of what he does not know and is terrified of change. Charlie Caucasian is that White man who will use code words to get his message out and when his words are decoded and exposed, then he forward some lame apology and excuse. He does things that under mind the progress of the Black man or any other group of people that is not his complexion and will come against those who are his color if their view is different from his. Mr. Charlie as I like to call him from time to time is that person who will quickly tell you that he is not a racist or a bigot, but will do all in his power to halter the progress of the Black man by a cold and calculated effort to under mine him and his efforts to bring about a positive change. Down through the years he has gotten fat because of his greed for more and feel that he is a dying breed because that which he have clanged to for hundred of years is slowly being distributed across the broad and he can't stop progress because many of his own kind is turning away from that heart of hate to a heart of love, not only towards the Black man, but all nation of people. He cannot bring himself to the point that he one day may have to relinquish that power that in his mind, has made him a god in this country. Mr. and Mrs. Charlie hate that this nation has elected a Black man to the office of the Presidency and they both fear that the day draws near that this country will fulfill the proclamation that Blacks has suffered for when it says equality and justice for ALL and not just for a select few.

Ch. 9 - So, what's wrong Black man? The Poem

So, what's wrong black man?
This is a question I ask of me, is a black man in this country really free? What is the view I see of me, do I fault the white man for the held back of me, or is it that of me who refuse to allow my mind to be free? No one can stop the growth of me, if I really, want to be free, only I have the power to stop me, but I can choose to be afraid of education and not be free. So this is the question, I ask of you, unless you to afraid, to be true. This is the question for us all, even to those behind prison walls. So, what's wrong black man? Answer your call, the action of you reflects on us all. Don't brush off this question, with the wave of your hand, answer the question and be a man. Do you see the life in your hood? Dope Thugs slinging drugs where Rev.Preacherman once stood. Preaching the gospel of GOD'S Holy word, but none of his street sermons have you heard, saying choose life and the way of right, flee from darkness and accept the light. So, what's wrong black man? Why is your face with that frown? Does the opinion the white man have of you, got you down? The time has come for you to make your stand; stop this hating on one another by helping the next black man. So, what's wrong black man? Have you lost your way? Have you forgotten all the positive things your parents would say? Things like learn of GOD; get your educational degree; respect other black men and raise your family. So, what's wrong black man? Have you giving up on life? You rather choose the wrong than to do what is right. Don't give up on life my brother man because things aren't going your way, make your strong stand, be courageous and have your say. GOD never said that

you will have a life of ease, but HE did promise to be with you if only you believe. Believe not the lie the devil say to you, for GOD'S word is real and GOD'S word holds true. Trust and believe is all HE asks of you and when tomorrow troubles come, HE will pull you through. So don't lose hope when it seems that life is to tough to cope, remember that you are here for a reason, trouble don't last always but only for a season. So, what's wrong black man? Have you said life is to hard and I've given up on myself; my education; my dreams and my hopes, all because in this day and time I can no longer cope, and I don't want a job so I'll choose the pavement and make my cream by the selling of dope. Making my cream is my dream and my bling has a high shine, whatever is yours I will come and take and yours has now become mines. You say in your heart I'm rolling in dough as you cook your crack just to sale more and your street given name is Clockin' Joe, killing young blacks as they smoke your blow. So, I'll ask again my Black man friend. So, what's wrong black man? Answer me in a complete sentence if you can, don't give me that lean excuse about being held back by the white man. He didn't put you on the streets to sale your death filled treats, that's a choice that you have choose, for that of yourself, smoking dope; slinging crack and selling crystal meth. Will you destroy my black sister's body and imprison that of her mine? Will you stop the progress of your brother as he does your jail time? So, what's wrong black man? Have you taken the time to open your heart and allow your eyes to see, just how your wrong is affecting, our black community? So, what's wrong black man? Do you even care about your black race and all the senseless killing that is taking place? Get an education; get a job and be that of a true man, uplift your brother and the community by the extension of your hand. So, what's wrong black man? You are killing your own kind; children are dying at school bus stops as the bullets come flying. They can't even walk the streets without the fear of being shot; they can't play little kids games, like marbles; jump rope or that of Hopscotch. Young black boys choose no school to expand their wonderful minds; they rather have money; cars; guns; and drugs and give high five to the street credit of being a Thug than to choose honor; respect; education and love. So, what's wrong black man? When you wear your pants down below your waist, do you even care about the look that Grandma has on her face and how others view you as being a total disgrace to our proud black race. So, what's wrong black man? Is the question I often ask of myself, do we as a people value the life of ourselves to the degree that when I see you that you are me? The actions of you are the reflection of me and I sometimes don't like what I see. I want you to be more than you dream you can be and when I see that you are who I dream you can be, than when I lie down at night and see your face and your actions is that of me, than I can say in the words that are true, that black man has become that of you. Do I now see a King, in this land called free or do I see another black man as a faded memory and if I look deep down inside, will I see a strong black man who will no longer hide? Embrace GOD'S love and welcome JESUS in your heart, for it's never to late for you to start. By the wisdom of GOD, you are here, to show the wonderful power of HIS hand, for you are destiny to be great, how I know this, for HE made you, a BLACK MAN.

So, what's wrong black MAN?

In Christ, J. Reid

Thank you page:

First and far most I would like to take this time to thank ALMIGHTY GOD for His grace, mercy and love that HE has bestowed upon me and for allowing me to write this book and to share my opinion, my view, my heart and my mind, for ALL glory and honor goes to HIM. Next, I thank my late father and mother, Seymour and Virginia Parker for loving me and giving me life. I thank my two daughters, Lateyia and Ashley Reid for listening to my idea and giving their honest opinion about my view and I know it has not always been easy. As I always told you both when you were kids, only Jesus himself love you more than I and I'm running a close second. I thank GOD once again, this time for blessing me with my three heartbeats. They are my three grandkids, Paris, Amaya and Jeremiah Reid, whom inspired me more to write this book perhaps more than anyone, simply because I want to give them a better start than I gave Lateyia and Ashley. To all my brothers and sisters, Seymour Parker 3rd, Cathy Harmon, John Parker, Alice Bell, Karen Reid, Minister Virginia Scott, William Parker and my late brother Bennie Reid, who made his earthly transition from this life to his heavenly home in the year 2005, know that I miss you and that I love you with all that is in me. My three brother-in-laws, Minister Christopher Scott, Levin Reid and Michael Smith. My three non- blood related sisters, Beatrice Parker, Leola Parker- Smith and my baby- sister as I call her, Annette Parker, please know that I love you all more than words could ever describe. A special thanks to my Aunt Dee Reid for always being in my corner even when some have chose to turn their backs and being more than an Aunt to me, for you are my second mom. To Bernice Savage, my dad's first wife, momma Chimmey I call her, thanks for treating me as your son, that mean a lot to me. To my cousin Bennie Smith, thanks for all the long and insightful talks on the phone and my truck-driving friend, Ralph "Shortman" Mears, you are truly a blessing and a true friend. Thank you for always encouraging me that I can do it and always having an ear to listen to what I had to say and talk about. To Bishop Audrey E. Giles, thanks for taking the time out of your busy schedule to read my book and wanting to write the foreword for me and to Dr. James J. Fedderman, I thank you for your friendship, for being an educator and for writing the foreword to my book. To you all, I thank you for believing in me when I told you all that I wanted to write this book and share my message with my people. To my brothers and sisters to whom I may never meet, I thank you for the purchase of this book and pray that it will bless you in some small way and last but certainly not least, I thank Trafford Publishing Company for taking a chance on this first time author and I pray that you, your family and any person that you may share this book with would have gotten something out of it that will help us as a people and a nation. THANK YOU MUCH.

Afterword

I do hope that this book will propel you as the reader to give some thought to some of the things that is written in this book and see that we have a growing concern in the black community when it comes to cultural conditioning and the problems that plague the black community as a whole. I want this book to be a tool that will equip you and your family with some understanding that you are a wonderful work of GOD's hand. This book is to educate you that you are not what you have done and that you are greater than what some may say about you. I want this book to encourage, equip, educate, empower, inform and uplift you as a person, a man and a friend. GOD bless you and your family.

Special Acknowledgements:

I would like to take this time to thank the followering people who continue to inspire me on a daily basis with their words of wisdom, their knowledge and their heart to serve their community so that we all will become a better people by wanting to be the change we so desperately need. They are as follow: Reverend Al. Sharpton; Joe Madison; Warren Ballentine; Steve Harvey and Willie Jolley. May the GOD of both heaven and earth continue to bless and watch over you all.

Conclusion:

Some of you may or may not agree with some of my opinions written in this book and I can respect that. The whole purpose of this book and its title is to get you thinking about the problems we face in this country as Black men. The advice given in this book is to bring us closer together as a people and I do believe that if we will take the time and truly listen to what is being said as you read the words, I truly do believe that you and I together can be the change that we want to see in the world. Read, Learn and Share the understanding, the ideas and the wisdom that is written in this book and apply it to your life and let it be an influence to how we should love one another no matter what color our skin may be and by doing so, you will see the changing power that Almighty GOD has placed in you and than you will become the true reality that our forefathers dreamed you could be. That strong, educated and proud Black man that he fought for you to be.

About the Author:

James Reid is the son of the late Seymour and Virginia Parker. He was born on Oct. 11, 1966 on the Eastern Shore of Virginia in the small town of Painter. He is a 1985 graduate of Nandua High School located in Onley, Virginia and the father of two daughters, Lateyia and Ashley Reid and the grandfather of Paris, Amya and Jeremiah Reid. He enjoys hanging out with both family and friends and love to host his memorial dinner that he puts on each year in honor of his mother. He is a person who loves to travel and does it for a living by driving an 18-wheeler up and down the East coast and parts of the mid-west of the United States hauling everything from produce to seafood and making friends on the way. He gave his life to Jesus Christ in February of 2002 after a bad decision that he made landed him in trouble with the federal government. He loves to share his faith with others and attend his church named Holy Trinity Baptist Church where he is a church trustee and an adult and teen Sunday school teacher. He is a faithful reader of the bible and loves to listen to talk radio especially that of Joe Madison; Warren Ballentine; Rev. Al. Sharpton; Willie Jolley and Steve Harvey. He loves talking to young kids about life when given the opportunity to do so and have a great love for people. He hopes that the love that Jesus has for him will be a light to those to whom he may encounter who continue to walk in darkness and no not why they stumble, especially the young people. He is a strong supporter of life changing charities where he is a faithful donor especially those who deal with kids such as "Feed the Children and Abandon Babies Charities." He believes that change comes by changing one life at a time. May GOD bless the reader of this book.

James A. Reid